Also by Walter F. Kern

Getting Started Riding a Motorcycle

50 Wild Motorcycle Tales

An Anthology of Motorcycle Stories

Walter F. Kern

Dedicated to Rosemarie

Contents

50 Wild Motorcycle Tales 5

Preface.. 12

1. Hell's Little Angel 13

2. Topsy-Turtle 13

3. Buzz Off.. 15

4. Chicken Caper 17

5. My Life as Evel Knievel (or Awful Kanawful) 18

6. You Take the Highside and I'll Take the Lowside.............. 20

7. Formation or Bust 21

8. How I Spent My Summer Vacation................................... 23

9. Give 'em Hell, Kid! 29

10. Biker for a Day... 34

11. Biker Scum... 35

12. Easy Testing 37

13. Coffee Caper.. 38

14. Leathers 39

15. Bike Buyer Bedlam 40

16. Lost on the Driscoll Bridge.. 42

17. Haunted Ride 46

18. Beartooth Pass.. 50

19. Riding, Icing and Sliding 52

20. Wheelstander... 55

21. The Plate Glass Window... 56

22. Old Harley / New Harley 57

23. "Chopper" Claus - Special Times 58

24. Be Prepared... 69

25. Touched By a Hells Angel 70

26. "Chopper" Claus - The Game 74

27. "Sturgis?" "Sturgis!" 81

28. Beet, a Diehard Biker 98

29. Afghanistan by Motorbike - The Dead Body 99

30. Afghanistan by Motorbike - The Relativity of Travel 103

31. Jailed in Afghanistan 106

32. I Remember How Scary It Was 113

33. The Biker 114

34. Attack of the U.F.M. 116

35. Song of the Rolling Sirens 119

36. First Kick 122

37. Sweet Revenge 131

38. Where There's Smoke 133

39. RawHyde Adventure 135

40. Safe Riding is No Accident 146

41. Don't Box Me In 157

42. The Coke Can 159

43. Trip to Llano 160

44. My Get-Off Got Me Riding 171

45. How I Got Back Into Motorcycling 173

46. 24 Hours 177

47. Drifting in France 183

48. On the Road to Namibia 196

49. Never Seen Rain 202

50. An Unlikely History of Motorcycles 204

Acknowledgments 209

About the Author 210

Preface

This book is an anthology of motorcycle stories. These 50 stories were submitted to the Motorcycle Views Website over a 13-year period by a wide range of motorcyclists from all walks of life. Some of these individual authors used their real names, others used nicknames, and still others used a shortened version of their real name. They each tell their own personal stories of what happened to them as they rode their motorcycles. Among these writers are a few professionals who made some of their works available to me early in their careers. They now have books of their own.

Some tales are very short, and some are very long. I've tried to mix them up. You may find the stories of some authors grouped together. Each tale was intensively edited to provide a good reader experience. You'll find humor, risk-taking, adventures, poetry, rhyming verse, 2-up excursions, world travelers, stupid tricks on bikes, lessons learned, winter riding perils, hazards while riding, and stories told by returning riders.

I wrote five of these stories myself. Two stories relate my experiences on my motorcycle trips. Two are fictional children's stories that involve fantasy and motorcycles. The last is a short fictional tale that describes an alternate world of motorcycles.

If you have a personal story of an experience you had riding your motorcycle, please write it up and send it to me for consideration in a possible sequel.

1. Hell's Little Angel

Back in 1973, I bought my first bike. It was a new Yamaha.

I was out riding one day by myself when, all of a sudden, all I could hear was the roar of engines behind me, two rows of them side by side.

As they closed in on me, there was something strange about them. It was me on my little 350cc Yamaha and all those bikers behind me, to my surprise, members of the Hells Angels, on their big Harleys.

So, I guess you could say that I rode with the Hells Angels.

It was quite an experience being surrounded by these guys. They nodded their heads at me as they passed, and I gave them a return wave.

It was the thrill of a lifetime!

—Keith Williams

2. Topsy-Turtle

I bought my first bike back in '64. I was 16. I got the same instructions all of us older bikers got when we were just learning to ride: "Down once and up four times; this is the brake; this is the clutch; twist here to make it go; and forget about the front brake, it'll get you killed." I had many wrecks on this bike. This is the story of just one of them.

I had been riding about four or five months, and thought I knew how to ride. I had already had several wrecks and had learned a lot.

I had also bought a car, a '56 Chevy, from my mom. Before she sold it to me, she had wrecked its front end. I needed to get the car repaired. A friend of mine was to pick up the car and take it to the shop for me. I was on my lunch hour and was riding to meet my friend at the shop.

We lived in the country, and it was hilly. The road had lots of curves. There was one curve that I liked. It was an "S" curve with a bridge in the middle of it. You rode down the hill into a right-hand curve, then across the bridge and up the hill into a left-hand curve, falling away on the other side. The posted speed was 35 mph. I was running it at 75. As I crossed the bridge and topped the hill, dragging pegs in the hard left hander, there, in the road, was the largest turtle I had ever seen. You know I hit him.

I can still see it all today. The bike straightened out and headed for the ditch. I had come off the seat and had lost my hold on the grips. I was to the left of the bike, in the air, headed for the ditch. I still remember the moment we—the bike and I—made contact with the ditch. I can still see the front tire and handlebars as they struck and twisted hard to the left. Then, as I rolled in the ditch, I lost sight of the bike—but not for long. As I rolled in the ditch, my own bike ran over me. We were both moving kinda fast. Then I caught up to it and ran over it. Then it ran over me again. I remember the dirt in the air, thrown up by the bike as I rolled over it one more time.

I wasn't wearing a helmet. There I was, lying in the ditch, both arms over my head, curled into the smallest ball I could make. I could hear the bike right behind me, still running. Waiting for it to make one more pass over me, I was still with anticipation. Moments passed, and then I looked. It lay there, twisted, but still running. What to do?

I walked to my house, about a mile back down the road. I called my boss and told him that I would not be able to come back to work as I had wrecked my bike and had no transportation. He asked if I was all right, and when I said I was, he informed me that he would send a tow truck for me and the bike.

Everyone had a good laugh when I showed up at work. I was scraped up some and bleeding from many scratches. I was dirty, and my uniform was torn to shreds. When my boss stopped laughing at me, he said, "Go get cleaned up and put on a clean uniform."

I think I did a lot of growing up that day. Not just because I had survived the wreck, but because, in spite of all that had happened, I had lived up to my responsibilities in my job and my life. I had started to become a man.

I got the bike fixed, but then, wrecked it many more times.

—Myles Bryant

3. Buzz Off

It was May, 2000. A group of friends and I were headed along the Blue Ridge Parkway (BRP) to do some bike camping. At the time, I had a V-Star Classic with windshield and all the trimmings (lowers, pipes, jetted, throttle lock, etc.). My helmet of choice at the time was an HJC Police Shorty with the storm curtain removed. Most of the time, I rode with ear plugs. My Roadhouse pipes could get a bit aggravating after awhile, as well as the constant wind noise. I liked the soft, orange bullet ear plugs, but I digress. Suffice it to say that I forgot to insert them back at the last overlook we took for a break.

There were six bikes in all, and I was next to the tail gunner. On a straight stretch of the BRP, two of my friends in the lead decided to "wick it up" a bit in a friendly rivalry of torque display. I had the speedometer humming pretty good in my attempt to keep up with them, when my ear was suddenly impacted by an insect. "Shoot!" I exclaimed. "I forgot to put my earplugs back in at the last stop!" "OK," I thought to myself. "Keep calm, slow the beast down and get it safely off the road." In the back of my mind, I was hoping that the tail gunner was also hauling his bike down so that he wouldn't rear-end me. Also, I couldn't shake the feeling that this was not going to end well and that whatever was jammed into my ear was bound to bite, sting, or bore into my brain at any moment.

Needless to say, I did a pretty good job of stopping the bike and moving it into the grass. I leapt off the bike and threw off the helmet so that I could assess my situation. My tail gunner had also made all the right maneuvers and was quickly by my side to find out what was going on.

There was a large, buzzing insect lodged DEEP within my inner ear. So deep, in fact, that the wings were physically beating against my eardrum. The sensation was freaky enough, but because it was so close to my eardrum, it amplified the sound to that of an angry bumblebee!

My friend pulled out a water bottle in an attempt to flush it out. As we attempted the flush, a camper van pulled over with an elderly couple in it. They too tried to help, but were at a momentary loss. A few minutes later, the rest of the crew had finally circled back in a panic, fearing that one of us had crashed. The lady returned from the van a few minutes later with some Swimmers Ear liquid drops, and we poured that into my ear. The (as of yet) unidentified insect went from annoyed to downright ANGRY, as this was alcohol based. However, the drops killed it in about three minutes. Again, we flushed the ear out with bottle water and hoped for the best. No buzz. No pain. I could hear very well, and we figured the insect was flushed.

Shaken and a bit weak, I boarded my bike and continued the rest of the trip without incident. A few days later after being home, I went to the doctor to check my ear. The bug was still lodged in my inner ear but in a crevice slightly above the eardrum where it did not interfere with sound. After 40 minutes of flushing with warm water and oil, the doctor was able to get it out in one piece. It was an ordinary house fly, and not a very big one at that.

The moral of this story is twofold: 1) always wear ear protection, whether it be from a full helmet, bandanna or ear plugs, and 2) always keep a level head in panic situations. Deal with getting the bike safely off the road, shut off and secured, first. Then deal with the situation, second.

—RedJacket

4. Chicken Caper

When I was in high school way back in the early '60s, I had a 175 Allstate. Back then, motorcycles only had two speeds to me: off or wide open. Of course, wide open was only about 65 mph on the Allstate.

Riding along a country road one day, I topped a small rise in the road and found a flock of chickens covering my path. It was too late to slow down, so I plowed right through them. When I looked back, all I could see was a white cloud of chickens and feathers flying in the sky.

When I got to my friend's house, he came out and said, "What's that on your muffler?" I looked down and found that I must have caught one unfortunate hen with the foot peg, and knocked an egg out of her. I had a perfectly scrambled egg splattered down my exhaust pipe.

—John

5. My Life as Evel Knievel (or Awful Kanawful)

I came of age in the rural south, where a driver's license could be obtained at the tender age of 15. You probably remember that time of life when your body has outgrown your brain.

Most boys of that era earned well under minimum wage. Our pay could be described as micro-wages, but, unfortunately, the term "micro" hadn't been invented yet. Buying any slick car was out of the question. Most boys ended up with some old granny-mobile that required extensive maintenance, and had no hope of attracting as much as a casual glance from the opposite sex. On the other hand, you could buy a great bike for around 500 bucks.

Envisioning myself as a ladies' man extraordinaire, I opted for the bravado of the bike. Situations like this help young boys develop important life skills, such as decision-making.

I decided to buy a dependable bike, not a hoopty, old car. Critical reasoning skills were also developed. Girls would rather ride on a bike than in a hoopty car.

Acquiring a bike at a young age forced me to learn another valuable life skill: persuasion.

Selling the idea to my dad was a monumental accomplishment. The adage about the squeaking wheel getting the grease is true. He finally gave in under duress, and allowed me to purchase a new Honda CL 100. Not exactly the CB 350 I was hoping for, but it turned out my old man knew more about what I needed for a first bike than I did. Imagine that, a grown man knowing more than a kid. It was a new concept to me at the time, but it taught me another lesson: go for the gold medal, but learn to be happy when you win the silver.

I rode that little 100 everywhere. Girls liked to ride, and I got quite good at handling the little bike. Pretty soon I started looking for new outlets to challenge my "awesome" cycle-handling skills.

One day a friend and I decided to go over to some gullies and do a little jumping. Evel Knievel was popular then, and I wanted to develop my stunt riding skills. We jumped a few gullies, increasing the amount of "air" we'd catch as our confidence grew. My friend gestured to a spot and suggested that I jump there. He was joking. The spot he suggested was unsuitable for what we were doing. This spot was unsuitable for anything related to a motorcycling activity. It might have been fine for training bulldozer operators.

I didn't bother to look at the jump site before making the attempt, so my friend didn't think I was going to do it. But, I rode back a little way, turned her around and took off. By the time I got close enough to the edge and saw what was before me, it was too late to do anything. (There is a lesson in here somewhere about looking before you leap. I just learned it beyond the point of no return.)

It wasn't the one-point front wheel landing, or passing through the brush pile, or hitting the pile of old bricks that hurt. It was my left forearm—between the rear tire and the fender—that hurt. The spinning rear tire gobbled up my arm all the way up to the shocks. I couldn't get it out. My friend couldn't either because he couldn't get up off the ground from laughing so hard.

19

I had two things on my mind, in this order: 1) get this bike off my arm and 2) carry out a Mississippi whoopin' on laughing boy. He finally recovered enough to help me extract myself from the bike, and we limped home with a broken clutch lever and broken ego.

I had just learned my first lesson in a series of lessons that all riders learn. The kind we never forget: humility. I decided that day that I would haul girls and leave the jumping to Evel. Eight bikes later, that philosophy is still working.

—Jimmy Presley

6. You Take the Highside and I'll Take the Lowside

I used to ride motorcycles. Then I gave up riding to raise my family. Now, I have reentered the world of motorcycles and have found it to be a very pleasurable experience. The bikes are bigger, faster, better, but that's not the best part. Information! You can learn anything and everything now.

When I was growing up, you had to ride 40 miles to Memphis, Tennessee to get a brochure about motorcycles at the dealer. Don't bother asking questions, because in those days kids didn't have any money, and, therefore, didn't need any information. We learned from asking older guys with bikes and got a lot of bad information that way, and we learned in the school of hard knocks.

In my younger days, the term low siding or high siding a bike were unknown to us. You just wrecked!

I gained some valuable information one Saturday morning when riding over to a friend's house. As I approached his place, I saw a group of our friends standing in the yard watching me ride up. I also spotted a plastic garbage can lid lying in the street. I had a thought: "Wouldn't it be cool if I locked the back wheel up on that garbage can lid and slid around sideways as I stopped?"

It sounded good in theory, but as I put the plan into action something went awry. I had miscalculated the speed of the bike and the frictional coefficient of the plastic material against the grain of the asphalt.

In other words, I busted it on both sides. Low side, High side, what's the big deal? I hurt on both sides.

—Jimmy Presley

7. Formation or Bust

Way back in 1985 I had just got stationed at Fort Rucker, Alabama, at which time I promptly bought a 1982 Honda FT500 Ascot from a fellow soldier who was leaving.

The first weekend I had the bike, I decided to ride it back home to West Virginia to show it off. Well, Mom (being a mom) promptly went out and bought me a full set of leathers. And, my girlfriend (being a girlfriend) kept me home much longer than I had expected. So in order to get back to the base on time, I had to be creative with my speed. I figured that when I hit Kentucky, I'd take the back roads where I could go faster because of the lack of police.

It was around 3 a.m. when I came upon these three sets of old coal mining tracks that were sticking up above the road. My first instinct was to hit the brakes, but I realized that there was no way to stop. I figured my best bet was to jump them, so I returned to full throttle. I damn near made it, but my back tire hit the very last track which then slammed my front end down and rocketed my ass-end skyward. Luckily when my back wheel hit the ground it was spinning so fast that it just slid around and passed the front wheel. By that time, I was on my back, sliding down the road at 100 mph, just watching the lights on my bike spinning round and round.

I still thank Mom to this day for those leathers. As for my bike, the entire right side was gone. My handlebar was flush with the tank, my foot pegs and rear brake pedal were mangled beyond repair and my exhaust system was straightened out and ripped off. And I still had hundreds of miles to go to make it back to base!

I still don't know how, but I rode it all the way to the base and almost made it in time for formation. But get this picture: I came rolling in on a bike that had no exhaust and no back brakes. I'm coming in hot and heavy, but I get the bike slowed down just enough that I was able to bail off right next to my company's formation. My bike didn't stop until it hit the barracks.

At first my sergeant chewed out my ass while everybody else just stood there in amazement. But after I told him my horrific tale, he said that I was one crazy son of a bitch and promptly gave me a day pass.

—ZOHAR

8. How I Spent My Summer Vacation

Every once in a while in life, opportunity knocks, and no matter what, you just have to answer. At least I do.

The company I work for has an office in New Hampshire and one of the women who works there recently married a man who rides, so when they came to my state, Florida, for their honeymoon last October, we made arrangements to meet in Daytona Beach at Biketoberfest. I only spent a few hours with them, so you can imagine my surprise at their insistence that I come up to New Hampshire for Laconia Motorcycle Week. I've been to most of the "big" bike events, but never thought I'd have a chance to go to Laconia. What better opportunity than to go with someone who lives there.

Making the decision to go was a tough one. I had to figure out how to get myself and my bike—my only bike ever; a '96 Harley-Davidson Heritage Softail I bought new—up there on a "shoestring" budget. Being a woman, and with many warnings received from friends about the northern traffic, riding by myself was not an option. So I borrowed an open trailer from a friend, and in spite of my trepidation about the condition of the trailer tires, hit the open road in my pickup truck with the bike in tow, way excited about my trip!

I had plotted a course where I would stop at my daughter's in Jacksonville, then at a friend's in South Carolina, and from there a mid-point overnight stay in Fredericksburg, Virginia, the only place I'd need a hotel room. I didn't even make it to Jacksonville before the "service engine" light came on in the truck. No problem. My son-in-law insisted I leave my truck there and take their new Honda Ridgeline. Now I'm stylin'!

I was on the road again next morning and made the scheduled stop in South Carolina with no problems. Had some "real" southern barbecue—which means hash and rice for those that don't know—

and left early the next day for the next leg of the trip. Things were going so smoothly I almost kept going past my scheduled stop in Fredericksburg, but after driving all day, I was ready for a drink and some dinner.

After I had pulled into the hotel, I discovered there was no place to eat, so I got into the truck again and drove a few blocks to Ruby Tuesday's. After dinner, I took the service road back to the hotel, and heard a distinct "clunking" coming from the trailer.

I looked in the rear view mirror, and saw the left wheel of the trailer wobbling to the point of almost coming off! At this point I was right around the corner from the hotel, but pulled right into an Exxon "convenience store" station to assess the situation. I looked at the wheel, saw a big "chunk" missing, and decided to call AAA. I dialed the number, and then, realizing I had no idea where I was, hung up and walked into the store to find out where I was.

Upon hearing my dilemma, my second "rescuer"—a very young clerk employed there—volunteered his tools and services to help change what I thought was a bad rim. Unfortunately, his wrench did not fit the lug nuts, and after several inquiries of customers at the pumps, I managed to borrow the proper wrench. Even more unfortunate was the discovery that it was not the rim that was damaged; it was the axle hub.

At that point, I thanked my store clerk friend, and asked if I could leave the trailer and truck there overnight, as there was obviously not going to be a quick resolution to the problem. I now had no choice but to "call home" in the hopes that someone would be able to help.

As luck would have it, the friend I borrowed the trailer from—much to my amazement—had a friend right there in Fredericksburg, and although he was working that night, he offered to come over the next morning. He arrived at 8 a.m. and after hours of searching for parts—and much anxiety on my part—a new axle, hubs and tires were installed on the trailer, and at 1 p.m., I was on the road again. What angel was looking out for me, not only that help was right there, but that I had stopped before the wheel might have come flying off at 75 mph!

I arrived at my friend's house in Nashua, New Hampshire at 11:15 p.m., and after socializing a bit, turned in for the night and readied myself for the "Big Day."

The next day, we unloaded my bike and put it in their toy hauler with their bike, and headed north for the one-hour trip to Laconia. They had planned ahead of time to park the camper in the driveway of a condo that some of their friends had rented for the weekend, so we were all set. I had my bike serviced before I left home, including a new battery, so I knew I wasn't going to have any problems. Little did I know the "fun" had just begun.

We left the condo on our bikes and headed into town. I needed gas, so we stopped on the way. After refueling, I hit the "start" button and was greeted with—nothing! No problem. There were plenty of people there to push-start it. Off to downtown we went, to get our HOG pins and watch the slow races. While there, we got a phone call that we had parked the camper on the wrong side of the condo, so we had to go back and move it. Good thing (again, luck on my side) after as we push-started the bike again and rode it the 10 or 12 miles back to the condo, there was a guy staying there who was a mechanic, and between my phone call—again—to home and this guy, it was determined the stator needed to be replaced. This was not a small job, particularly with not many tools. But had we not gone back to the condo, we could have done a lot more damage to the bike had I kept riding it. I have to tell you that it was at this point I finally got discouraged, and began to question myself for even attempting this trip.

I decided to put the bike away and consider what little bit of riding I had done "enough." But my friend's husband wouldn't have it. He insisted that we call the closest Harley dealership in Meredith and take the bike in. Of course, when he called, their "take-a-number, it's first-come, first-served" attitude reinforced my earlier decision. Not one to give up so easily, he called Heritage H-D in Concord, a mere 30 miles north, and at 4 p.m. they said, "Sure, bring it on in. We may not get it finished today, but you can pick it up in the morning." My logical side knew I could bring the bike home and get it fixed for half of what I would pay up there but if I did that, then I trailered it all the way up there for nothing. So we borrowed a trailer, and off we went.

We stayed at the dealership long enough to find out that it was not only the stator, but also the voltage regulator. It would not be ready until the next morning, and I was to call the dealership at 8:30 for a progress report. I called at 8:30, and they said two more hours. In the meantime, everyone's waiting.

Knowing that everyone was sympathetic, still didn't keep me from feeling like crap. Here I was, someone they didn't even know, keeping them from spending their time doing what they came here to do: ride.

I called the dealership at 9:30 for an update, since it would take almost an hour to get there. Much to my surprise, the service writer said, "It's done. Unfortunately, we had two incidents beyond our control happen when the mechanic took it out for a test drive. First, the left highway peg fell off. He retrieved it, and it was fine. Second, one of your saddlebag lids flew off. He got it back, but not before considerable damage was done."

My anger over these two unfortunate incidents was quickly diminished by my relief at not hearing that he had wrecked the bike. At least he got the lid back, so no matter how bad it was, it was fixable and far easier than trying to replace a 1979 FLH saddlebag. I told him we were on the way, and suddenly realized that these things had to have happened due to all the bouncing over the 1300+ miles I had traveled. I ran this by him, and asked him to please look over the entire bike and make sure nothing else was loose, and he agreed.

When I arrived at the dealership, the service writer looked me in the face and told me he checked the bike over himself, and everything was tightened down and ready to go. The lid was not as bad as I had anticipated, but still required fastening to make sure it didn't come off. Finally, I was "on the road again!"

About halfway back to the condo, I looked down and the highway peg was spinning around. In his usual spirit, my friend's husband got his tools out again, and tried to resolve the problem. The dealership had reinstalled the highway peg with a bolt that was too long. I told him to let it go, everyone was waiting, but he insisted on trying to fix it. He got on his bike and took the bolt to a nearby marina and had a mechanic cut it down. As luck would have it, it was the wrong bolt entirely, requiring another trip to the hardware store, but it was finally done, and we were ready to ride.

We had two long rides scheduled for the weekend. One was a trip around Lake Winnipesaukee, and the other was up through the White Mountains along the Kancamagus Highway. Since part of our day was already gone, we chose the lake ride. It was one of the most beautiful rides I've ever been on—truly spectacular, and well worth everything I had endured to make it happen.

Saturday morning, we set out for the mountains. We had gone less than 20 miles when I realized things were not right. The bike was getting louder and louder, and by the time we found a safe place to stop, the muffler had come completely loose. We had no tools with us whatsoever, but we had pulled into the parking lot of a small post office, so my friend's husband went inside to see what we could borrow. In the meantime, I phoned the service writer and not-so-tactfully advised him where I was and WHY. It was not a nice conversation.

My friend's husband returned with only a wrench, not enough to get the pipes back together. After several attempts, he said, "If I only had a screwdriver." Then, an elderly gentleman walked over with a leatherman's tool. He had stopped at the post office on his way to take his grandchildren home, and helped us get the muffler back on and tightened up. The children had never been on a motorcycle before, so they sat on my friend's bike and we took their pictures while the repairs were made. We thanked him profusely, got back on the bikes and headed up to the mountains.

After ten miles or so, we came to a stop sign, where I pulled up beside my friend's husband, and said, "What a beautiful road!"

He looked back at me and said, "You've got another problem." (Is this story ever going to end?)

We crossed through the intersection and pulled into a fire station, where I discovered that my lights had been going on and off since we left the post office. I was not comfortable heading up into the mountains without knowing what was wrong, so we called the dealership and they promised to get the bike right in. We headed back to the dealership where a new service writer helped us. The first one never said a word or even acknowledged I was there again. After waiting three hours, we were advised that they found three places in the wiring that were corroded, and they thought they had resolved the problem. I thanked them, paid them, and we headed back to the condo.

Most of the day was now over, so we parked the bikes for the night and took their truck into Weirs Beach for our last night there. Next morning, we loaded their bike into the toy hauler, and I rode mine back to Nashua.

I probably rode a total of 250 miles in New Hampshire, but what incredible miles they were! And what a great time I had!

And what I learned:

1. Worse things than flat tires can happen.
2. The kindness of strangers can be totally overwhelming, when you least expect it.
3. I do, in fact, have a guardian angel.

At every biker event, I look for a new souvenir pin, and always have a problem choosing one. This time, I found it right away—a beautiful little pewter pin, "Laconia 2007" with an angel on it!

—Deb

9. Give 'em Hell, Kid!

Many of you have never heard the term, but Scrambles was my first try at organized motorcycle racing.

Back in the mid '60s, the tiny town of Pinehurst, Idaho held a Scrambles race most Saturday afternoons. We couldn't do it on Sunday because Smelterville held the Hillclimb on Sunday. You did not need to join anything or sign anything. All you had to do was show up. There were two classes: 250cc and below and open class.

I finally wore my dad down, and he let me enter. He rode a Yamaha 100 Twin—it was street legal—from our house to the "track." Mom hauled all of her kids, dogs, and beer in the Scout.

The riders meeting was chaos with kids chasing dogs, dogs chasing kids, and moms swatting kids. Essentially the rules were simple: cross the hayfield, hit the old skid trail into the woods, ride the ridge to the top, and back down the draw to the hayfield and the finish line—and do it five times.

The tricky part was staying on the right side of the ribbons across the field so that fast and slow riders were not racing head-on.

The riders ranged in age from seven to 70. Just to make it interesting, sporting, or perhaps more deadly, anyone over 16 started in the second row, facing the wrong way with engines off. There were perhaps 10 of us under 16 and twice that many over 16. So, we young'uns lined up behind a rope held by two volunteers who would drop the rope on a signal from the starter.

Fathers scurried up and down the line, making last minute checks to see that their kid's bikes were running. Dogs darted across the field. I saw the rope twitch and all hell broke loose.

Being on the outside of the front row, when I prematurely popped the clutch, the guy holding the rope was yanked into my bike because he had the rope wound around his hand, and it was now between my fender and front tire. I fell down. He fell down. The kid beside me fell down. The rest tore across the field while the starter yelled, "WAIT, WAIT, GODDAMNIT WAIT!"

They managed to get the kids back in line. Dad picked up both me and the bike while the rope holder glared at me.

Dad put the left side mirror in his pocket and said, "Give 'em hell, kid!"

I stood on tiptoe revving the 2-stroke, teeth clenched in grim determination. The flag dropped. The rope holder beside me threw his end of the rope and ran backward. Bikes rocketed from the line. I stood on tiptoe revving the 2-stroke, mouth open in confusion because the bike wasn't moving.

As the first of the senior riders whipped past me, I slammed the bike into first gear. In retrospect, I should have used the clutch. This would have given me a bit more control but with the throttle wide open and no clutch engaged, the Yamaha launched upward like a missile. My death grip on the handlebars gave it a pivot point as it stood up, twirled to my right, and chased the rope holder into the crowd of lawn chairs, beer coolers, and spectators scrambling for their lives.

The rope holder shrieked as he grabbed the handlebars from the opposite side, tripped over a cooler, and held on to wrestle the bike to the ground. I pushed the helmet up off my eyes in time to see Dad put down his beer, and lift the bike off the hysterical rope guy. He set the bike upright, pointed it across the hayfield, kicked it into life, stepped off, and leaned the bike toward me.

"Give 'em hell, kid!" he said as I crawled back on.

The other riders were disappearing in a cloud of blue smoke as I roared onto the field, clinging to that bike for dear life. Halfway across the field, I speed shifted into third, holding the throttle wide open with my right hand, trying to push the helmet up off my eyes with my left just in time to see a small creek disappear beneath the front wheel.

The front wheel cleared the ditch, but the rear hit hard, catapulting me over the bars, and the bike tumbled backward into the three foot deep ditch.

I rolled and then scrambled back to my feet, pushing the helmet back, looking for the bike, and finally spotting it in the water. I squirted into the creek to find the bike mostly upright, leaning against the bank enough that I could right it and jump on the kickstarter. It fired, and I popped it into gear, moving down the creek looking for an exit.

The helmet bounced up in time for me to spot a shallow bank, and I turned hard right, flogging that engine as hard as a nine-year-old could. I felt the front tire lift, and then I was in the field, throttle wide open, speed shifting, pushing the helmet up with my left hand, grinning as the ribbons flashed by on my right! ON MY RIGHT?

This was probably the first time in my riding career (although certainly not the last) that I remember thinking, "Oh @#$%, this is gonna hurt!" The leading riders were returning across the hayfield, mere yards away, aimed directly at me! I could see the grin of the lead rider turn to a grimace as he realized he was playing chicken with a nine-year-old with nothing to lose, least of all my dignity.

He hurled his bike sideways, slamming into the front wheel of his nearest follower as I tried to pull myself up on to the seat enough to roll my right wrist forward and SLOW THIS DAMNED THING DOWN. I leaned hard right, trying to get back on my side of the field as the thundering herd began to gather around me, metal screaming as riders gaped at the mud covered apparition cutting across their bows.

Alas, my side of the field was no sanctuary as many of the riders detoured to avoid the growing pile of twisted metal. Motorcycles were flung to the side as riders dove into the dirt and at last I had a clear shot to the end of the field and the skid road.

I roared from the scene of the battle into the coolness of the jack pines, bouncing from kelly hump to kelly hump, juggling my helmet. The little two-stroke screamed as I gave it no mercy, twisting and turning, jumping, not with grace, but sheer desperation, as I topped the hill and turned downward toward the hayfield.

A long straight beaver slide led into the field, allowing me to hit fourth gear, and the helmet bounced upward enough so that I could see the speedometer needle twitching spasmodically over the 60 mark. I screamed across the field, catching glimpses of men and machines lying about, as if resting from a day spent bucking hay bales.

Then I saw the Ford pickup. It represented the turn at the end of the field. I downshifted hard. I slid up toward the tank, blipping the throttle, hitting the brakes hard, preparing to power slide around, and begin my second lap.

I blame the crash on my helmet. I truly believe that if I could have seen where I was going, I would have slowed sufficiently to make the turn. I went into that slide a bit hot.

Around the back of the Ford, I was in good shape, but it began drifting on me. I rolled on the throttle to straighten the bike and pulled myself out of the slide. I might have used a bit too much throttle. The Yamaha began to scream. So did the spectators.

The first beer cooler exploded in a shower of ice and glass as bottles were hurled into the air. An aluminum lawn chair crumpled as an over-sized lady was thrown backward. The back wheel slid out more, and I knew I was going down.

I blame the dog for the high side that followed although I can understand his inability to flee. He was blinded by beer, his tail trapped beneath the fat woman and the lawn chair. The rear wheel struck him, the bike flipped, and I flew through the air.

As I sat up amid the moaning aftermath and pushed the helmet up off my eyes, I could see the rope guy glaring at me and hear my father's drawl, "You gave 'em hell, kid."

—Curt Patterson

10. Biker for a Day

Brad and I have been friends for many years. In the summers, if I stopped by, he would always come out and admire my bike, sit on it, and then tell me how he hoped to get one for himself, someday.

A couple of weeks after Christmas, Brad called me and insisted on me coming to see what his wife, son, and daughter got him for Christmas.

I went to Brad's to see his Christmas present. We had a couple of glasses of rum and visited. Finally, we went into his garage and saw his Christmas present: a new motorcycle.

It was a combo street and trail bike—brand new, shiny, pretty, no dirt or dust. To me, the bike looked like a monster bike (very high seat).

Brad got on it and started it up. He had a grin like a Cheshire cat. I don't think anyone could have been happier than Brad on that day.

"Wanna see me ride it?" said Brad. He didn't wait for an answer. To my knowledge, Brad had never before ridden a motorcycle until he got this one.

As he took off, he almost stalled it—in with the clutch and more throttle. The front wheel came off the ground about three or four inches, but that didn't stop him. Down the road, he went.

He turned around and came back past me showing that big grin. He turned around again and rode back and into the garage.

Brad sat on the bike in the garage with the motor still running. He thought it was in neutral. He let out the clutch, and it jumped. Then, in with the clutch, but why he gave it more throttle, I will never know. The clutch came out, and the bike stood upright like a flag pole.

34

Somehow Brad landed on his feet, both hands still on the handlebars. The motor was still running, and the bike did two spirals on its rear wheel while standing tall. Then, Brad lost it, and the bike came down with the handlebars crashing through the windshield of his wife's Corvette.

With the motor still running and the back wheel spinning, Brad was able to open the car door, reach in, and hit the KILL switch, shutting off the motorcycle. Then, his wife heard the commotion and entered the garage.

Like a true loving wife should, she asked, "Are you hurt?"

He answered, "No."

Then and only then, the proverbial #$%@ hit the fan!

Now, this was my chance. I hurried out the garage door, got in my car, and left.

Time has gone by since this event. I hope Brad is still alive. I'm not sure, as I am afraid to call.

Brad was a biker for a day. I'm sure he loved it.

—Edeee2

11. Biker Scum

Roadside Diner, just up ahead
In front, a primo spot
Backed in my scoot

Laughed at my boots
'More dirt than leather,' I thought

Wasn't exactly very well scrubbed
Been one hell of a long, hard ride
A burger sounded good
And, if need be, guess I could
Take my grub and eat it outside

Once inside, those classic stares
That sets me all aglow
Was it, 'No Good Bum'
Or 'Biker Scum'
Which touched my heart just so?

The 'ol waitress who worked the joint
Probably from day one ...
Thought, for sure, was gonna shout
'Grab yer gloves and get the hell out!' ...
Smiled and said, 'Help ya son?'

I smiled, she winked, told me, 'Pay'em no mind
Yelled, 'NUMBER 2, MEDIUM WITH SPUDS!'
She gave me a Coke
Told me a joke
Said, 'Sorry hun, ain't got no suds'

She took a break and sat by me
reminisced awhile
About a son
Her only one
How I kinda had his smile

Her eyes welled up, as she went on
Of how he loved to ride
I held her hand

Said, 'I understand'
'It's a feeling deep inside'

Orders were up, she had to go
'I too have to run'
On my way out
She barked at the crowd
'GOD LOVE THAT BIKER SCUM!'

—Laurence P. Scerri

Editor's Note: Larry's book, *Asphalt Range*, is available at
www.asphaltrange.com and contains this poem.

12. Easy Testing

In 1972, I was living in Fairfax County, Virginia and riding motorcycles for a couple of years, mostly through the kindness of others taking pity and being brave enough to trust me with their machines.

It was time to buy my first motorcycle, a 1972 Honda CB360, and become a licensed rider.

I went to the DMV, got the book and started studying. I dutifully and eagerly learned it all and could execute perfectly the figure 8, winding through the cones and everything else required.

An older friend, Alan, had taken the test on his 125cc Honda and lived close to the DMV office in Fairfax and said it would be easier to pass using his 125 and would meet me there on the test day with the bike for me to use.

Well, the day came, and I nervously took the written test, passed and followed the instructions to bring the bike to a designated spot in the parking lot.

Outside, Alan and I waited with the bike for the examiner. The examiner came outside, called my name and told me to pull in behind the car he got into.

I started the bike to follow him as he pulled out, but my friend said, "No. He wants you to wait here until he comes back."

The examiner and car drove out of sight, and I removed my helmet and waited.

Twenty minutes later he came through the door with papers in hand and I started to get ready to go. But to my surprise, he handed the papers to me and said, "You did great, but I must have lost you in traffic."

The words were on the tip of my tongue, "But I ..." He turned and went back inside, and I've been riding ever since.

—Jim

13. Coffee Caper

Well, it was around 1971 or so and a nice Saturday morning. I was on a ride in Orange County California, near John Wayne Airport.

I was in the left lane of a highway, just passing a car, when the guy in the car tossed out a cup of coffee. I got a face full of it! It had cream and sugar.

I looked over and could see the guy had on a pilot's uniform, and a stewardess was riding passenger.

I came up with a retort to his action, but I wasn't mad. It was too nice a day for that. I let them pull ahead, and I wiped the coffee out of my face.

I caught up with them at a red light a minute later, rolled up alongside, stopped, looked over and said, "Hey, I like my coffee black!"

He looked at me, somewhat startled, and then looked at her. She giggled and then he said, "I'll try to remember that next time."

At that, I started cracking up, and we were all laughing.

I just waved and took off, grinning.

—Airhead

14. Leathers

My leathers have been with me since I started motorcycling. I tend to wear them whenever I'm riding.

They are faded from the elements, stretched and saggy from use, but they still keep me from taking abuse.

My leathers bear the scars, scrapes and abrasions from a few slips and spills. My leathers still keep me warm from those morning chills.

Despite them being my bodyguard, we have become old friends, going on long rides together, taking on hills, valleys and bends.

My leathers have sheltered me from the rain and the fog. They even have blocked the bite of an angry dog.

They have protected me from flying rocks and bugs and have been on the receiving end of many hugs.

My leathers have shaded me from the blistering sun on a long, dry and hot Texas run.

Over time, they have become as supple and comfortable as a broken-in boot. As a bonus, there's a place for my gun in case I need to shoot.

My leathers are getting old, wrinkly, and slightly tattered, but they continue to protect me from getting battered.

They have screened me from the wind, and they will stay with me to the end.

But at the end of this long ride, it's not just a cow's hide, it's my skin.

—Torch

15. Bike Buyer Bedlam

I'd had my first bike—a little red 1971 Honda CB175—for a good six years, setting a trend of hanging onto my rides for a long time. I had ridden it from the suburbs of Pittsburgh into school in the city every day the weather allowed, south to Tennessee via the Blue

Ridge Parkway, around several of the Great Lakes, as well as to East Coast seashore locations. It had been dependable, economical, and lots of fun, but eventually the desire to step up a bit in displacement and performance persuaded me to make a move.

Being on a rather restrictive budget, I was going to have to get a heck of a deal, and that is indeed what came about. The Shriners' motorcycle corps up in Erie was upgrading to something new so their fleet of 1975 Honda CB550s—in pristine condition and equipped with custom four-into-two exhaust—were up for sale. If I could sell the 175 and resort to my bank's write-yourself-a-loan program, I'd be in business.

But, I needed a buyer. It turned out my brother-in-law, Kurt, was in the market. I hadn't thought of asking him if he might be interested as he didn't seem the adventurous type and had no experience with motorcycles, but a sale is a sale, so we agreed on a reasonable price, which I recall was a hundred bucks less than I'd originally paid for it.

We got the tax, title, and license plate legalities all cared for and then it was time to introduce him to his newly acquired machine.

He put on his helmet, lifted his leg over the seat and onto the foot pegs, turned the ignition on, pulled out the choke, pressed the clutch lever all the way to the grip, put the gearshift in neutral, lifted the sidestand, and then—with a bit of hesitation—pressed the start button. The little engine fired up immediately. All was well, to that point.

"Give it a *little* gas and *ease* out the clutch," I said. Those were the simplest, most concise, instructions I could think of...

Well, straddling the bike with both feet on the pavement, he gave it the gas—more than a little—and dumped the clutch. The bike left without him! Kurt was left standing there, still on his feet, while the bike headed maybe fifty yards down the street before falling over.

One of us hit the kill switch and then we assessed the damage. The only real damage—other than to pride—was a broken off clutch lever, but it brought a tear to my eye as I thought to myself, "What have I done? I got hardly a scratch on the bike in six years, until now!"

We got a small vice grip and clamped it to what was left of the clutch lever. It would do for the moment. The riding lesson would now continue in the back yard where there was soft grass and fewer obstacles.

This time he got it going smoothly enough, but perhaps some more instruction on braking would have been in order. As speed increased, panic set in, and the bike and rider went into the side of the house, leaving a dent in the aluminum siding (that remains as a souvenir of the occasion, all these many years later).

Kurt didn't stay with the bike for very long, hawking it for the cash needed for an engagement ring. It was probably a better choice.

—Revh

16. Lost on the Driscoll Bridge

My wife, Jane, and I had attended the Americade Rally in Lake George, New York since 1994. It was just 270 miles from our house in New Jersey. We were going again this year, our thirteenth consecutive Americade Rally.

We had our two Honda Gold Wing 1500 Motor Trikes—Jane had a white 1998, and I had a red 2000—serviced before Americade. Jane went on a ride with our local GWRRA Chapter NJ-F (F-Troop) in early May, and the alternator went out. She had to get the bike towed back to our local dealer on a flatbed. A new alternator was installed. With any luck, we should now be set for the riding season.

Another complication that year was the onset of arthritis in my shoulders and hands. It started during the Polar Bear Grand Tour season and was still being evaluated by a local arthritis specialist. The result was a lot of pain at times that I'd never had before. I went in for two cortisone shots in my shoulders. Getting old is not fun but it is bearable so long as I can keep riding motorcycles. So, all my rallies that season were test cases to see how I would hold up with the new infirmities. In addition, Jane had a bad knee that most likely would require surgery after Americade. She had a lot of knee pain and got her own cortisone shots before we left.

We were up at 6 a.m. the day we left for Americade. We had a quick breakfast, and then did some last minute packing and loading of the trikes. We were out the door on time at 9 a.m. and headed for a gas stop.

We traveled up to the entrance to the Garden State Parkway just south of the Driscoll Bridge. As we rounded the entrance ramp to the Parkway, I noticed a sea of nearly parked cars across six lanes of traffic heading for the bridge. This traffic mess was not good news.

We threaded our trikes into the stream of traffic. Jane was just ahead of me maybe two car lengths. I moved to lane three and lost sight of her. I called Jane over the CB to ask her what lane she was in. Dead silence. I called again, and again, and again, and got no response. Where did she go?

I couldn't see Jane's trike anywhere. Did she have an accident? Was she ahead of me somewhere? I felt panic.

I went over the Driscoll Bridge among six lanes of cars and threaded onto I-287 West. All the time I kept calling for Jane over the CB. There was still no response.

I traveled down I-287 about eight miles and didn't see her anywhere. Finally, I pulled over to the shoulder and took my helmet off. I tried to call her on my cellphone—all I got was voice mail. I waited and waited and still no Jane—just truck after truck flying by at 65 mph.

We had long had an agreement that should we get separated, the one in the lead would pull over and wait for the other. She was ahead of me the last time I saw her, but I had not seen her. Maybe she was still behind me, and I had missed her somehow. I had to go back and look for her.

I turned around and headed back over the Driscoll Bridge peering over into the other direction of traffic looking for her trike. I saw nothing. I got over the Bridge and pulled to the side of the road. I got out my cellphone and tried to call her again. I got a voice mail again. I was in a panic now.

I decided to retrace my steps, so I turned the trike around and headed back over the same route. Just then I heard my cellphone ringing in my pocket, and I pulled over to the side of the road and yanked off my helmet. The ringing stopped.

I tried to call her again, and this time, she answered.

"Where are you? Why didn't you wait for me?" I said.

"I'm at the rest stop in Morristown, waiting for you," she responded.

Well, I was furious (and also very relieved). All I could do then was ride the trike to the rest area where everyone else was waiting for me. We were now 45 minutes behind schedule.

We finally all got together and headed north to the New York Thruway. About half way to Lake George, I could see traffic stopped ahead of us. We gradually slowed down, finally coming to a stop. From there, we inched along for more than 30 minutes.

Switching to CB channel 19, I found out that an accident had occurred involving three fatalities. An accident investigation team was on the scene, and that had slowed traffic to a crawl. Will we ever get to Lake George?

The previous year we got half drowned in thunderstorms trying to get to Americade. This year we delayed ourselves because we couldn't keep track of each other on the Driscoll Bridge. Then we got further delayed because of the heavy traffic associated with this accident.

We did get back some lost time when we got to Lake George since we were so late to registration that all the lines were gone, and we moved through quickly.

It was always something that created drama for us as we rode to Americade. We've never had an uneventful trip. We've had a medical emergency, a dead battery, a broken driveshaft at 70 mph, thunderstorms, pollen invasion, and a near riot in the street. This particular year it was the dreaded 12-lane Driscoll Bridge.

Keep us in your prayers for our next run to Americade. You can also listen in to us on your CB (if you're near us on the road) as we converse with each other. Our friends tell us that we're a riot to listen to.

—Walter F. Kern

17. Haunted Ride

The workings of the road are stranger than the workings of our minds. The roads less travelled are usually the ones that take us places, but may lead us into the unknown.

It was the end of an insignificant winter this year. My house had burnt down following an electric short circuit which had claimed the life of my beloved dog and companion. Unable to fix my mental fortitude, I decided to head out for the hills of Shillong, my home town, to regain my composure. Little was I to know that the pine covered hills would offer me a very different welcome this time.

Having fixed and repaired my house, I got out my Royal Enfield Thunderbird, packed the essentials and set off on a fine sunny day. It was to be a 100 km ride to Shillong and then another 100 km to the border town of Dawki.

With the heavy construction work along the Guwahati Shillong Highway, NH40 was a mess of dust, rubble and potholes. As I reached near Shillong, the skies turned dark grey signaling the inevitable downpour that was on its way. Turning up the throttle, I raced towards the hill town hoping to arrive at my favourite restaurant before the storm began.

With lady luck on my side this half of the trip, I managed to find a comfortable seat at the restaurant just as it began pouring outside. The temperature suddenly dropped, and the weather got quite chilly. But the charm of eating a steaming hot plate of chicken gravy with my favourite Thai fried rice while it poured cats and dogs outside was unrivalled.

I was prepared to beat the weather at its own game this time. With my stomach full of a heavy dose of protein and carbs, I got into my waterproof gear and fastened my helmet on securely. With a quick prayer, I kick-started the T-bird to life and headed off towards the Bangladesh border.

The rain was incessant. There wasn't a moment where it relaxed its wet grip over the trip. I kept climbing up Shillong peak, careful as streams of water crisscrossed over the asphalt, in gentle trickles at places and as gushing waterfalls at others.

Wetness got a new meaning in the very first hour. My waterproofing gear was being tested to its vertex. But I found the Enfield to be super reliable even on the trickiest of places where it muscled through muck, oncoming gushing water, and steep inclines. There was just no stopping it. It felt as if it had come to a life of its own in the storm. It was in its own element.

With the thunder crashing all around, the Thunderbird seemed to be living up to its name. Riding nonstop for two hours, I had left behind the road that heads towards Cherrapunjee. I was now close to Pynursla, a small town on the road to Dawki.

A well-deserved cup of hot tea found its way to my table as I stopped at a roadside tea stall. A few cups of tea and some locally made biscuits rejuvenated my spirits but didn't do much to aid my freezing hands. The rain had finally tired down, and had resorted to becoming a gentle, but unwelcome drizzle.

Dawki wasn't too far away now. The scenery, however, changed drastically. The dark green pine forests had given way to a lush green, super-dense jungle which towered over the road, which had grown narrower. Everything was much darker than usual. It became very quiet with the forest muffling out noise. The lack of human habitation was obvious. The sun set far more quickly than I had anticipated and soon I was riding in pitch black darkness.

I had accessorized my motorcycle with HID headlamps, dual 55 watt fog lamps, and dual hazard lights. Visibility was not my problem. The twisting jungle road seemed endless, and my eyes were wide open to discern dangerous branches that were having a gala time hitting me at every turn. However, something felt wrong.

I stopped the bike to check the time and realized that I had been riding for nearly four hours. Dawki at best was only three hours away from Shillong. I had probably lost my way, made a wrong turn in the dark or took some road where I had probably missed a turn. But I had been on this road before, and I couldn't think of any place where I might have got off the road and lost my way.

Now the forests around Dawki are well known to be infested by venomous snakes. I wasn't about to risk being bitten standing here in the middle of God knows where, and decided my best bet was to keep heading down the road. I was bound to come up to some form of human settlement. So off I went riding at an average speed of 40 kph to maximize fuel efficiency. I didn't want to be stuck out here without fuel.

After about half an hour of riding, I came across a house with a clearing around it. The house was completely dark. Having seen a million horror movies, I felt this might be the perfect hideout for some psychopathic killer or worse. But I braved my chances and went up and knocked on the door.

No one answered. I turned back to look at my bike. The T-bird was shining in the moonlight, the sky now bearing an innocent star studded look. I knocked once again and then started walking back towards the bike. It was then that I felt something.

For a moment, I felt as if I was hallucinating. I had walked up to my bike and got on it and looked back at the house, but I could no longer discern it in the darkness. It was as if the forest had swallowed it. The moonlight breaking through the tree tops kept shifting. I tried to convince myself that the long ride, the cold, and this darkness were each playing tricks on my mind.

I looked away. Now I couldn't make out the road. In the dim moonlight, I could make out the dense forest on my left and a grassy field broken by wild bushes on my right. I got off the bike, bent down and touched the ground in front of my tyres. Cold, wet grass greeted my near frozen fingers. I stood up looking for the road. It was nowhere.

Now, I always had an interest in the paranormal but here, I seemed to be living in it. I wasn't scared. My curiosity had overpowered my fear, and I was looking out into the darkness slightly enjoying what I believed to be a complex form of hallucination. Then something moved to my right. I spun around trying to make out the shapes in the dark. Then I saw it again. It was a little child whose silhouette was clear among the bushes, and he was not alone. I saw at least five more figures running around hiding among the bushes only visible when they would run across the moonlight. Now since there was no possible way that small children were running about in the middle of a desolate and dangerous forest, I jumped on my bike to get the heck out of there.

I turned the key and hit the start button, my eyes glued to those creatures, whatever they were, hiding behind the bushes, but the bike refused to start. I hit the start button again. The engine whined but stayed cold. It was then that I felt something brush against my right boot. With a reflex action, I kicked out and swung open the start lever and kicked the lever hard. The T-bird blasted into life!

My hands automatically found the switches to the HID lights and the high powered fog lamps. Instantly they shone before me, burning up the darkness as the roar of the Enfield engine tore through the blanket of silence, sending resounding thumps into the wilderness. My eyes broke through the veil of pitch black unknown and there I was, standing in the middle of the road, no house in sight, no grassy field, but only the defeated forest on either side, at least six feet away from the road. I could feel the hot engine between my legs as I pushed the bike into gear and sped off forward. I reached Dawki an hour later.

Next morning, with the breaking of dawn, I headed back to Shillong. As I crossed the forest, now bathing in the early morning sunlight, I tried to decipher the events of the previous night, which now seemed more like a dream.

It was then that I looked down and noticed the grass stains on my boots and clothes...

—Saurav Bhattacharjee

18. Beartooth Pass

It was August of 1993—the year of the great Midwest Mississippi floods. My wife, Jane, and I had traveled out from New Jersey to our first motorcycle rally. It was a Rider Magazine rally held in Cody, Wyoming. While at the rally, we missed the guided tour of Beartooth Pass. Jane said she just couldn't ride 6000 miles and not see Beartooth Pass since we were only a few miles away. So we started out on our own.

The roads were good for a while, but then I saw traffic stopped ahead, and I started slowing down. I stopped behind a car towing a trailer. A Wyoming state road employee was holding a stop sign up ahead. I was on my 1990 Honda PC-800 motorcycle. My wife was immediately behind me on her twin PC-800. We had ridden up from Cody after an overnight rain had stopped.

After waiting for five minutes, I could see cars moving. I pulled in the clutch, jammed my left foot down to engage first gear, let out the clutch, gently rolled on the throttle, and began following the trailer ahead of me. That was to be a mistake.

Almost immediately I knew something was wrong. The road surface was becoming soft, and then it was mud. I realized that the drivers ahead of me had misinterpreted the signal of the person holding the sign and had taken the side of the road that was under construction. This mistake was no big deal for the cars. It was a giant mistake for anyone riding a motorcycle. My bike was now swerving. Then I thought of Jane behind me. I looked in my rear view mirror, just as she fell.

I leaned forward in the saddle to look in my mirror to see what had happened to Jane. She was sprawled in the mud about 50 yards behind me. She and the bike had parted company. I then became aware of my own situation.

I was still moving, but I needed to stop. Hopefully, I wanted to stop upright. All I could think of was the training I had received in my courses and the tips I had received from other riders. I gradually began applying the brakes gently so as not to lock up any wheel. I had to steer so as not to allow the bike to fishtail. Somehow, I got the bike stopped and my feet down in the mud, upright.

I slowly turned the bike to the left and across the gravel median to the other, paved, side of the road and headed back up the hill toward Jane. My tires were coated with mud, and they were slipping. I didn't know if I would make it back without falling down myself but, somehow, I did.

I parked on the side of the road opposite Jane and moved her bike across the median to my side. Jane was OK but covered with mud. We always wore helmets, leather jackets, and gloves, so Jane had no perceptible injury except bruising. We just had to get all the mud off her and the two bikes. We decided not to continue to

Beartooth Pass but to head back to Cody where we spent the rest of the day washing down everything and relaxing.

We had started out from New Jersey as a party of five on four motorcycles. Somewhere along the way, we had split up. We were going to have to ride the 2500 miles back to New Jersey on our own. We had some damage from the adventure trying to reach Beartooth Pass. Jane had some lingering injuries, and her bike had considerable plastic damage. We had to order new PC-800 body panels and have them delivered to the dealer in Bloomington, Illinois. We would be stopping there anyway to visit Jane's sister on the way back.

When we got back and related our stories, our kids couldn't believe our adventures. Our daughter Sue said, "Most parents worry about what their kids are doing. In this family, the kids worry about what the parents are doing."

—Walter F. Kern

19. Riding, Icing and Sliding

This story took place in December, 1972 while I was stationed at Ft Hood, Texas and was 19 years old. Back then you had to wear a helmet in Texas. I remember this incident very well, have not exaggerated or embellished it, and I even remember the names of the other riders.

It was a Sunday afternoon, and three friends and I were returning from a weekend in Dallas. I was solo on my CB 450 in the rear, with John W. on a CB 350 Scrambler (driver and passenger) and Kenny N. on a CB 500 solo up front. We rode those little bikes everywhere. They seemed like real road machines then. Normally we had no problems.

However, on this day, there was a sudden severe storm developing, and we were on I-35 South refusing to exercise good judgment and stop. It was one of those times where the temperature dropped 30 degrees in a couple of hours. It was raining, turning to sleet, and the temperatures were dropping rapidly, but we were cold and wet and decided to push on and get back because there was no other good option, or so it seemed at the time. We were riding very carefully of course—can you believe this? Does it sound like a typical recipe for disaster?—Duh!

Icing began just south of Waco. The helmets with face shields were at least keeping our faces from freezing. The daytime speed limit then was 70, and we were doing at least 50. Somewhere just short of Temple, spaced out and running with the flow of traffic, the CB 500 was going over a bridge (a culvert overpass) and just went down before my eyes. Boom! Wow! It happened so fast (no skid). It seemed like it just collapsed. Next, the 350, with passenger, went down. Oh-Oh. I had no time to brake or swerve (plus I was numb from the cold). Physics was totally in charge.

As soon as I hit the bridge, I went down too. So there we were, four people, three bikes, sliding down the bridge on a sheet of ice like glass. We, indeed, had a problem, but a bigger potential problem was—as I noticed as I went round and round on my back—the semi bearing down on us from the rear and cars behind him sliding all over trying to regain control.

As I was spinning round on the ice, I watched the driver of the cab-over semi sliding left and right across both lanes, heaving on the wheel and trying to slow it down without jack-knifing. I experienced that slow motion effect. I was trying to kinda swim a backstroke on the ice in a desperate attempt to get to the shoulder, but just kept going straight along with the rest of the pack—the things you do when you are faced with a do-or-die situation. We slid along for what seemed like forever, finally stopping spread out across the two lanes. The bikes slid a bit farther than we did.

Somehow, the truck and the cars behind were able to stop just past the end of the bridge where we all came to a halt. The trucker certainly did a fantastic job in controlling that rig. We immediately jumped up and dragged the bikes off the road—wasn't hard at all. The trucker took off straight away as he didn't want to get rear-ended. A state trooper (DPS) showed up in about 45 minutes as we stood there forlornly freezing. He had us sit in the cruiser to get warm, and he had the base call a couple of his friends who had pick-ups, to come get us. (Since all we had between us were a few bucks, a towing service was out of the question.)

Now this is what still amazes me to this day. It was so icy on that bridge. How icy was it? Well, it was so icy that there was not so much as a scraped turn signal, handlebar grip, or foot peg on any of the bikes. Other than our clothes being wet, you could not tell that we had been sliding along the road. And, nobody even had a bump or a bruise. In fact, the trooper just assumed we had stopped out of good sense, and was amazed when we told him what had happened. Also, my friends had never noticed the semi until it was over as they were not spinning as I was and never thought to look behind.

I did learn from that experience to watch bridges in general for icing, to not ride motorcycles in icing conditions, and to always wear a helmet. I'm convinced that my helmet saved me from a severe head injury in 1972, and that's why I have always worn one, to this day.

—Jeff Ross

20. Wheelstander

My mate Craig had just got his motorcycle learners permit, at the ripe old age of 30. In this state, a learner rider is limited to riding bikes up to 250cc capacity for the first year. Craig couldn't wait to buy his first bike, and insisted on buying a showroom-new one, despite my suggestions that an old "pre-loved" bike would make more sense. (The guy was hopelessly uncoordinated, and I suspected that he would be making a few close inspections of the asphalt before getting the hang of things.)

Now Craig weighed in at around 220 pounds, so I was keen to see what he looked like perched atop a little 250cc bike. I went along with him one sunny Saturday morning, testing bikes at various dealerships.

He wobbled about on a variety of small road bikes, not looking comfortable or in control of any of them, and as the day progressed a feeling of impending doom began creeping up on me. With each new bike tested, Craig looked more and more wobbly. I also noticed his habit of putting both feet flat on the ground while waiting at traffic lights, a bad habit which later in the day would come in handy for him.

At last came the fateful test of a Kawasaki ZZR250—a bland, somewhat underpowered little machine. Perched on it like a hippopotamus on a kid's dinky bike, Craig tottered out the driveway of the dealership and pulled up at the traffic lights, his feet flat on the road each side of the bike. I could see him clearly from the dealership window, and I watched aghast as the inevitable tragedy unfolded.

The traffic lights turned green. Craig opened the throttle, dropped the clutch, and got it all wrong. The little bike reared up like a stallion, tore out from between his legs, wheelstood on its own across the oncoming traffic, and threw itself down on the opposite sidewalk. I half expected it to burst into flames (I watch too many movies), but it just lay there resting. Meanwhile, Craig was still standing exactly where he had been at the traffic lights, his arms comically still in the "handlebar" position, his legs still crouched as if the bike were still under him. He hadn't moved so much as an inch. I can only guess at the look on his face, but I would give anything to have seen it.

The dealer was very kind about it all. He was more impressed than angry, because a ZZR250 is utterly impossible to wheelstand— Colin Edwards couldn't do it. We had just witnessed a miracle of physics.

—Chris Shaw

21. The Plate Glass Window

I got my first motorcycle in 1982, a Kawasaki KZ440. I had never ridden before, and the dealer gave me minimal training. I left the dealership and went about 100 yards, where I had to either take a right or a left. I could not find the brake, so I went straight ahead where I hit the curb. I was going fast enough that I hopped off the bike and ran a few steps without falling. After I had traveled five or six steps, my progress was stopped by a building.

This was not an ordinary building. It was a very busy restaurant with large plate glass windows. My first contact with the window was with my helmet. The rest of my body was close behind, until I was in a spread eagle position against the window.

The window made a terrible sound but did not break. I peered in the window and was surprised to see virtually all the diners looking at me. Apparently, the noise inside the restaurant when I hit the window was even louder inside than it was outside.

In the background, my bike was revved up, lying on its side with the wheels not touching the ground. Embarrassed, I quickly picked up my bike and got the heck out of there.

—John

22. Old Harley / New Harley

Being fairly new to riding, I knee-jerked and bought myself a 2002 Harley Sportster XL1200 Custom. Well, my father had a '76 Harley Sporty that he enjoyed—the ones made by AMF. The shifter was on the right, and the brake was on the left. Well, we were riding up to Brasstown Bald in North Georgia from Griffin to spend the night. I'll never forget that trip!

About halfway up there, I allowed my concentration to drift while navigating stop and go traffic. I looked up just in time to slam on my rear brake and skidded up to within an inch of a Dodge van's rear bumper. Dad pulled up next to me, and I shouted to him, "It's OK, I did that on purpose!" He looked surprised, but I swore he was utterly convinced that I did it on purpose.

Along we rode, and we had a repeat. This time it was a Ford pickup—I was getting tired—and I told him, "My brakes felt spongy, and I was just checking them out. They're fine."

Well, we stopped ahead, and he decided he wanted to ride my bike to see if it was OK, not knowing that I wasn't used to his shifter being on the "wrong side." I never even thought about it.

It took me two seconds to figure it out, and we continued on. I still made the mistake of shifting with the British-styled controls (right side), and braking using the left foot pedal.

57

Once again, I did my stopping trick (almost hitting a Camaro), only THIS time because I wasn't used to his bike.

He looked over at me and said, "I KNOW my brakes are good. Would you please stop showing off!"

I never said a word.

—Greg

23. "Chopper" Claus - Special Times

This is a fantasy tale of "Chopper" Claus, long-lost brother of Santa Claus. Chopper—no one remembers his real name—helps his brother by overseeing the design and production of toys at the North Pole factory. He also assists in the delivery of toys on Christmas Eve. Santa relies on Chopper to also conduct in-the-field research regarding new toys that should be added to the production line. Chopper is also an avid motorcyclist (biker) except right now he has no bike at all. All the time that he is helping Santa, he is always thinking about motorcycles.

In this story about Chopper Claus, he takes off some Special Time to visit a friend's family trying to find out what new toys he should make for next year.

There are two weeks in the year when Chopper Claus can take trips on a motorcycle. This year he wanted to do something different. He wanted to visit some kids and get their ideas for new toys. He decided to go after the first snow fall and visit his longtime friend and motorcycle buddy, Johnny Presents. Johnny used to work with Chopper as a Santa's Helper. (Don't you think he had a great name for someone who makes presents?)

58

Johnny had many children, and they always wanted new and different toys. They even called Chopper their "Uncle."

It would be a perfect trip. Chopper didn't have a motorcycle right now so he would take the Polar Express train from the North Pole. Right after the trip, he was expecting a surprise that his elves had promised him.

Chopper called Johnny Presents on the telephone to confirm the time he would be arriving.

Johnny was sitting on his motorcycle at a stoplight when his cellphone rang. (His personalized ringtone was "Vroom Vroom Vroom.") He reached in his jacket, pulled his phone out, and answered it. "Hey, Chopper, what's up?" said Johnny.

"I'm just about ready to make my trip to visit you and your kids," said Chopper. "I'm scheduled to leave on the Polar Express train at noon and should be there tomorrow at eight a.m. I know your kids well, and I always enjoy myself when I visit. They don't follow me around like I'm a rock star. I can just be myself around them. I want to ask them about what new toys they'd like to see me work on for next year."

"They are looking forward to your visit," said Johnny. "I'll meet you at the station. I know you're looking for toy ideas, but do you plan to bring some new toys with you that you've been working on? You know, to get their reactions?"

"Yes, I have a few new ones I'll bring," said Chopper. "It's just too bad we can't get some riding in this time. I enjoyed those twisties down Route 7 the last time I was there. I'm without a bike right now, and I'm suffering from Parked Motorcycle Syndrome. Maybe the kids will just let me relax and forget about my lack of a bike. See ya tomorrow Johnny."

The stoplight had changed for Johnny as he replied, "Got to run. Traffic is moving. See ya in the morning. Have a great trip."

Johnny arrived at the train station the next morning just as the Polar Express pulled in. He watched the passengers walk down the steps leading out of the train. After a few minutes, the smiling face of Chopper Claus emerged through the doorway carrying a green bag over his shoulder.

"Hey, big guy. How's the bike running?" said Chopper.

"I knew you'd ask about the bike first since it used to be your bike," said Johnny Presents. "Good thing you were getting a new Ultra Classic and were kind enough to give me an opportunity to buy your old bike."

"I just wanted to make sure it was going to get a good home, and I'd have a chance to see it once in a while," said Chopper. "How are those great kids of yours?"

"The kids are fine and anxious to see you. What's in the bag, man?"

"Just the toys I told you about. How's your wife?"

"Sandy's OK. Just got out of the hospital," said Johnny. "I'll tell you about it later. Hop on the back of my bike. It's only a mile or so from here."

"It feels great to have the wind in my hair again," thought Chopper. He thoroughly enjoyed the ride in the brisk air. Finally, they turned into a tree-lined drive leading up a slight incline to Johnny Present's house.

Chopper followed his friend through the front door and stood there in the foyer with the bag of toys tossed over his shoulder.

"Hey kids, it's me!" said Chopper. There were screams of joy as Johnny Presents' kids ran through the house and jumped all over their Uncle Chopper.

The children in Johnny's house had just got up out of bed and were still dressed in their pajamas.

Six-year-old Caroline, with her long golden curly hair, had on her favorite pink nightgown. She ran up to Chopper and yelled up at him, "My Daddy painted my room pink just for me. I have a pink dresser, pink bed, pink bedspread, pink pig, pink pillow, pink phone, pink ..."

"Wait a minute there Caroline," Chopper interrupted. Then he spoke in a soft voice to his pink friend, "Do you want a world all filled with pink? We need more colors than pink. And please don't yell, sweetie. You'll wake up your Mommy. You need to be quiet. Shh!"

"I know, but I like pink. Pink, pink, pink. Did you bring me anything pink?" she asked.

"Sorry, Caroline, but I'm low on pink this year," he said. "So I guess you want me to make more pink toys for next year. Is that right?"

"Pink is for little girls," said Caroline.

Her eight-year-old brother Connor interrupted with, "Girls are stupid."

"I am not stupid! You're stupid," returned Caroline.

"Please kids, I'm here to get your help about what you think I should make for new toys next year," said Chopper. "We can't do that if you're going to fight with each other."

"Well, I'd like to see a pink motorcycle," said Caroline. "My Daddy's motorcycle is all green and chrome looking. I never see pink motorcycles. When I get old enough to ride, I'm going to paint my bike pink. I think that we need to have pink motorcycle toys now to get people thinking about big pink motorcycles when they learn to ride. What do you say? What do you say? Please. Can you make some pink toy motorcycles? And, please leave me one next year for Christmas."

"Hard to argue with a six-year-old, curly-headed girl with her mind made up," thought Chopper. "I'll see what I can do."

Chopper took off his coat and sat down on the floor next to three-year-old Ian.

"Ian, I have something here for you to play with," said Chopper, pulling out a set of blocks from his bag and placing them on the floor in front of Ian.

"I like blocks," said Ian. "We have them at school."

Chopper knew that Ian was in pre-school now, and they had lots of educational toys to play with. He knew that blocks—some of the first toys—were still widely used both to entertain and educate kids.

"What do you do with your blocks at school Ian?"

"I play with them," said Ian in his tiny voice. "I build houses and bridges and towers. I stack 'em up and knock 'em down, boom."

"Do you learn anything with the blocks Ian?" asked Chopper.

"I learned my ABCs and numbers from them," said Ian. "Mommy helps me make words like cat. That's C-A-T. And numbers like how old I am. That's 3. These blocks you brought me don't have numbers, only letters. How come?"

"Well, these are good for spelling words, but they don't help much with numbers," said Chopper. "I need to make two sets, one with letters and one with numbers and then pack them together. Would that make a good toy for next Christmas?"

"I like blocks," repeated Ian.

Chopper knew that kids liked blocks. He knew that Ian wasn't much of a talker yet, but he would be, especially if he got more toys that he could learn from as well as knock down.

"Ian," said Chopper, "You've been a big help to me. Keep the blocks, and maybe I'll have a lot more for you next year."

Connor came over to Chopper and tugged at his sleeve. "Get up Uncle Chopper!" said Connor. "Go outside with me and ride on the new sled I got."

Chopper got up slowly. His arthritis was acting up again. "Let me put on my coat first," said Chopper. "It's cold out there."

"My Dad bought me this sled, but it's pretty big," said Connor. "You could put you and me both on it and your bag of toys too."

They went out the front door and found the sled leaning against the fence. Connor ran over and dragged it to the top of a hill next to the front porch. "Come on Uncle, let's go, and go fast," said Connor excitedly.

Chopper was used to sleds. After all, he had the biggest sled in the world, except it was designed to fly through the sky and not slide down hills. They got on the sled and Chopper placed his toy bag in front of him. Connor grabbed a toy bell out of the bag and sat down in his Uncle's lap. Then he started ringing the bell.

That gave Chopper an idea for a new toy. He remembered that his mother used to call him home from play by ringing a cowbell out the front door. Everyone in the neighborhood would hear it, and someone would always make sure to tell him it was time to go home.

"I'll make a new bell for mothers to call their kids home from play," he thought. Then he remembered that these days hardly anyone is even out playing in the yard. They're all into soccer, dance lessons, karate, cub scouts, after-school sessions, watching TV, chat rooms, blogs, texting, iPads, and smartphones—no time for old-school playtime.

"Kids still seem to like sledding though," he thought. "Connor, how about I make a smaller sled with pockets to hold your iPad, smartphone, and a small TV?" said Chopper.

"Sounds great! Whee!" said Connor. "Down the hill we go!"

After only two runs down the hill, Chopper was tired and decided to go back in the house to warm up. He took off his coat again and placed it on the hall stand. Just then, he heard a scratching coming from the front door and went to investigate.

He slowly opened the door just a crack and around the edge of the door appeared two noses followed by two sets of glowing eyes. A puppy and a kitty bounded into the foyer.

"What have we here?" said Chopper. The kids all came running in upon hearing their Uncle's cries.

"What a cute puppy," said Caroline.

Connor ran over to the kitty and picked it up. "This one's mine," he said.

"Where's my animal?" said Ian. "I want a snake."

Chopper then remembered that two of his own pets, Golden Boy and Gray Ears, had been messing around with his green bag while he was placing the toys in it that he was bringing on this trip. They must have climbed in the bag and fallen asleep at the bottom.

"Now kids, these are your uncle's own pets from the North Pole," Chopper said. "I guess I've found another gift that would be very welcome for next year. They aren't toys though. You can't stuff them into a corner and forget about them. They need care and lots of love. I need a new Santa rule. I won't bring them to children unless I get letters from their parents saying that their children are responsible and will take good care of them."

"That's a good rule," said Connor. "I'll be nine years old next year, and I'll be much more responsible then. I hope you'll be bringing me a present that is alive. I want a kitty just like Gray Ears, here in my arms."

Chopper got the green bag and the two animals climbed back inside and got all cozy.

Chopper heard a faint cry from somewhere. Then it got louder.

Johnny walked into the room with his wife, Sandy, on his arm. "Uncle, I told you my wife had been in the hospital," said Johnny. "She had a baby girl and now they're both back home."

"Hi Uncle," said Sandy. "Here's my new bundle of joy, Andi. She hasn't got to the all-pink stage yet, but she seems to be taking after her sister Caroline, so it won't be long."

Both Johnny and Sandy seemed like kids again as they made baby sounds and fussed over Andi. She was beautiful in her all-white gown.

"Want to hold her?" Sandy asked Chopper. "She may be our last baby. The family is just about the right size for us now. Four kids and four motorcycles are enough to keep us occupied."

Chopper took the tiny baby in his arms and looked lovingly in her eyes. "What a peaceful child," he thought.

"Children are the best part of Christmas," said Chopper. "They are the future. They just have to fill their minds with knowledge and be taught to be responsible human beings. Then they need to learn how to get along with all kinds of people all over the world. It's a difficult job that all parents have to assume. I know you two will do your part, and I will do my part. If only we could convince the rest of the world to do the same."

"I think I'll be giving an extra present to each child next year," said Chopper. "I'm going to whisper the words 'peace be with you' in every sleeping child's ear. Then, maybe, they will be peaceful children, just like Andi. I've learned a lot on this trip, and I'll be taking many ideas for new toys back to the North Pole. I'm still waiting to hear from my elves about their surprise for me. I wonder what it is?"

Chopper walked into the den and sat down in a big overstuffed chair, in front of a blazing fireplace. The kids were playing on the floor, and baby Andi was with her parents on the couch.

"What's that on the mantel?" said Chopper. "It looks like one of those old-fashioned snow globes." He remembered that he once made a big batch of snow globes and gave them to his closest friends. He worked long and hard to get all that snow in there.

"Well, I got it from you back in 1990," said Sandy. "The kids love it and it has a likeness of you in it with a few animals including a polar bear and a penguin. Of course, I know that penguins mainly live at the South Pole while polar bears live near you at the North Pole."

Chopper got up from his chair, picked up the snow globe, and gently sat back down in the chair again. He turned the globe over and watched it fill with snow. Then he turned it right side up and watched it snow all over him and the animals.

"It makes me homesick," he said. "I've only been gone a few days yet I feel a need to get back to my work. And, I'm very curious about what the elves have in store for me. That surprise is getting to me. Would you mind terribly if I cut my trip short?"

"Not at all Uncle," said Sandy and Johnny, almost in unison.

"Listen Chopper, I'll take you back to the train station in the morning," said Johnny. "But you'll have to ride on the back of my bike again. No, wait. Why don't you ride the bike and I'll ride on the back?"

"That sounds real good to me," said Chopper. "I'm itching to ride my old bike one more time."

The next day, Chopper was on the Polar Express. The elves met him at the North Pole station, with a surprise. They crowded around Chopper as he got off the train. The elf known as Midnight spoke first.

"Chopper, we all wanted to help fulfill a dream you had a year ago," said Midnight. "Remember when you told us you wished you could get a chopper like the one you'd seen on the TV show, *American Chopper*?"

"I remember," said Chopper. "But we have to spend all our money buying materials to make our toys. We don't have much money left over."

"Well, we heard all about your trip and the new ideas you now have for toys," said Midnight. "We think that future Christmases will be even better than before. It's your dedication and energy that makes the Christmas Eve run possible. We also think you need to be able to get away for Special Times."

"I appreciate your kind words, but I couldn't do it at all without the help of all the elves," said Chopper. "But what's this all got to do with the chopper I was dreamin' about?"

Just then another elf skipped over to a garage door and lifted it, revealing the surprise.

"*American Chopper* built this chopper free, just for you," said Midnight. "They will be showing how they built it on their TV program in January."

It was the longest, baddest chopper that Chopper Claus had ever seen. The pipes almost dragged on the ground, and it had a flame paint job and big saddlebags for all his stuff. There was even a little room for a few elves if they wanted to hitch a ride.

"Start 'er up!" said Midnight.

Chopper couldn't believe his eyes. He took his coat off, put his leg over the seat, switched on the ignition, put it in neutral, and pushed the start button. "Vroom Vroom Vroom" the engine roared as he twisted the throttle.

"I love that sound," said Chopper. "Now I can throw all my energy into making next year's toys knowing I have my own special toy."

Then, he looked at the license plate. It read: "Special Times"

—Walter F. Kern

24. Be Prepared

My first bike was a Kawasaki GPz 550, and it was one of the greatest bikes for a beginner.

Originally, I found a great deal on another bike and even left a security deposit on it, but I had to get a friend to pick up the bike with me (no license yet). When we returned, the owner apologized and said his buddy had cash and had beaten me to the house by 45 minutes. God was watching over me that day. The bike was a 1987 Yamaha FJ1200.

So I learned to ride my dependable GPz in 1990, and commuted almost every weekend between Fort Ord, California and San Mateo, California—about 100 miles. I used to pull off the road, and take my helmet off, because it was only required on the base— it didn't look cool on the road.

On one Friday afternoon, I was running late to get to my girlfriend's house, so I didn't have time to stop and remove my helmet as I was speeding up Highway 156 between Highway 1 and Highway 101.

There is a spot in Hollister where the two lanes merge into one, and I decided to speed up to get ahead of a bunch of slow cars. As I looked over my shoulder to watch the cars fading in the distance, I returned my attention to the road ahead and saw a gray van. Within seconds, I noticed I was catching up to the van much faster than I thought. Then, I realized that the van had stopped and had no brake lights.

I hit my brakes and scanned my options. There was gravel on the right and an open lane on the left with no on-coming traffic. With the rear tire locked, I glided my slide to the left side of the van, and just as I thought I had pulled off this save, the van made a left turn.

I didn't drop the bike but lost the right side panel, dented the tank where my knee was pinned between it and the van's fender, and put my helmet through the glass window above the rear tire.

I learned a lot from that experience. First, every biker has to expect that he or she will have an accident. It's the smart riders that don't put themselves in positions that increase those odds. Second, always wear a helmet. Helmets are cool. Third, be careful what bike you ride. If I had been on that Yamaha FJ, who knows what would have happened.

—Richard

25. Touched By a Hells Angel

Things settled down after they called me stupid—a fitting name—although not my most coveted term of endearment. They had to say it just to show they cared, and once they got their two cents in, they put more restraint in their comments:

"Well, there goes the family name," relatives said.

"We're circling the drain."

"Yeah, and I'd say it's already flushed down the toilet."

"Oh, God, what next ... tattoos?"

No, to put it mildly, my family was not delighted when I purchased, at age 50, my first motorcycle, a 2003 Harley-Davidson Dyna Wide Glide complete with Anniversary Gold Key Package, Accessory Studded Seat, and Vance & Hines Custom Long-Shot Neighbor-Waker Pipes.

70

My cultural deterioration started last summer, a year ago when, at my wife, Joanie's class reunion, I struck up a conversation with a gent sitting by his lonesome in the corner of the banquet room. "You look like you're inherited," I said. He gave me a quizzical look. "I mean, you look like the spouse of someone who's enjoying their class reunion. Lemme guess: aside of your significant other you don't know a soul here and you're tired of listening to the funny old stories, none of which you were a part of, or find any humor in whatsoever."

I had guessed right. Bill and I struck up an instant friendship, talked the rest of the evening, and agreed to get his wife, Sonja, and Joanie together. "But not next month," he said. "Cuzz, as of next week, I'm gone for 30 days. I'm goin' to Sturgis, South Dakota for the biggest motorcycle rally in history—a million bikes. Then I'm touring the whole country—7,000 miles on my Harley-Davidson Road King. Don't wanna fuss with razors or haircuts so I'm shaving my head the day prior to departure. Whatever grows, grows. Wanna come?"

What! Did this guy take me for some low-life idiot? Of course, I wanted to come! But there was a slight hitch. I didn't have a motorcycle. Nor did I have a motorcycle license. Nor had I been on a two-wheeled vehicle since I was fifteen, and that was the human-powered type. The truth is I'd wanted to ride a motorcycle ever since I had a brain, even if it wasn't the finest version of one.

But my family loathed the idea. Could I blame them? Statistics say you're about nineteen times as likely to do the bucket on a motorcycle as opposed to in a car. They say that staying safe on a two-wheeler requires triple the focus. I agree with that assessment. But then again, the motorcycle is a triple vehicle.

A motorcycle is 100 percent bicycle, 100 percent convertible and 100 percent fun. Nothing provides such freedom, exhilaration and camaraderie with the outdoors as a motorcycle. It's an in-your-face connection between the world and your senses. It's the bark of your exhaust, the windy rush, the carve of a curve, and the perfume of nature. You plow the horizon, unfiltered by the sterilized, automatic, window-tinted, air-bagged, climate-adjusting, traction-controlled, sound-deadened cage we call an automobile. You can "bet-chur-bippy" I wanted to ride! Without ever admitting it outwardly, I had secretly wanted to ride for 50 years. But would I ever do so?

Keeping it to myself (because #1: I knew it would delay the "you're stupid, you'll kill yourself" comments, and #2: I might chicken out), I took the first step: getting a learner's permit. I studied and passed the written exam then spent the next month like a pesky neighbor kid, borrowing motorcycles from very nervous friends.

30 days later I passed my road test on a rented mini-scooter that I could practically carry under my arm. License in hand, I headed to the dealer to check out 700 pound machines. My visit was an opening experience. It opened my eyes and my wallet. A five-day 30-hour safety course, called Rider's Edge, was available. Determined to make a fool of (or as others described it, "kill") myself, I signed up.

A few weeks later that fall, I found myself in a classroom with several other similarly stupid individuals. We spent half our time indoors, learning the physics. The other half we did outdoors on bikes, applying the principles in the field. The instructors didn't sugar coat it. They described all the risks, broadcasting them in morbid living color via video. Then they taught us some ways to reduce the risks—surprising information.

For example, we practiced "countersteering." You see, when you want a motorcycle to turn right, you turn the handlebars left: weird, but a principle of Newtonian physics that works (untrained bikers do it, but don't consciously realize it). We covered emergency braking. Motorcycles are different from bicycles: long story short, the cruiser's back brake takes your life; the front brake saves it—enlightening stuff.

I walked away from that experience with three thoughts: 1) I learned a whole lot, 2) Motorcycling is scary, and 3) I want to do it. By spring I'd done my research, gone shopping, and made my purchase. You might say it has changed my life!

I am now a confirmed chromaholic, adding new parts on a strict seven day schedule. I'm a member of the RETREADS® (over-40 club), the local H.O.G. (Harley Owners Group®) and a top active participant with the Motorcycles.About.Com forum on the Internet. I have four helmets, two pairs of chaps, five riding jackets, a leather vest, half a dozen dew-rags, and a plethora of accessories spilling over the shelves in the shed.

Joanie says that when I suit up to go out on my rides, I look like someone she's not sure she wants to be associated with. Well, we might look "bad," but my riding buddies are a retired state trooper, a school teacher, an insurance salesman, a civil engineer, and a certified public accountant—not exactly Pagans, would you say?

What's with the Hells Angels and the Pagans, you ask? Best I can tell, the old gangs have mellowed a bit. Yeah, there are some hard cases, but my limited experience has been: don't bother them, they don't bother you. Substance abuse has lost popularity, too. The profiles have changed a lot. Attitudes don't align with looks anymore. Education and safety training have become cool. And being a good brother (or sister) to your fellow rider is the code of the road. In fact, go to a motorcycle rally today and look past the attire. You'll meet the greatest, nicest, most regular folks you can imagine. Throughout my training and subsequent travels, I've encountered nothing but pure help and moral support from fellow riders. I've made some first-rate friends, too. Motorcycling is a kinship unlike any I've ever been involved with, and I'm thoroughly enjoying it.

73

Times are changing. Things are changing. Why then, shouldn't you and I? Is there something you always wanted to do but held back? Want to go in a different direction, find a new style, a new way, or a new idea? Could it be you've been an adult so long it's time you became a kid again? Or maybe you've spent your life acting like a big baby, and you're considering the scary concept of growing up. Maybe it's that secret thing you always wanted, but feared wouldn't line up with others' expectations. What is it you wish for, just before you blow out those birthday candles? You had better do it. Or go to your grave regretting you never tried. My friend, the world re-writes itself every day. What's the big crime if you or I veer onto a fresh new road? Now is a great time to start. Will some accuse you of being stupid? Of course! But once you've done as many stupid things as I have, you get used to it.

P.S. So far I've managed to keep the rubber side down, and my family is grateful I didn't get that skinhead tattoo. But, the other day I saw this groovy belly-button ring and...

—R. Denny Blew

26. "Chopper" Claus - The Game

This is a fantasy tale of "Chopper" Claus, long-lost brother of Santa Claus. Chopper—no one remembers his real name—helps his brother by overseeing the design and production of toys at the North Pole factory. He also assists in the delivery of toys on Christmas Eve. Santa relies on Chopper to also conduct in-the-field research regarding new toys that should be added to the production line. Chopper is also an avid motorcyclist (biker). All the time that he is helping Santa, he is always thinking about motorcycles.

Chopper Claus had filled his sleigh at the North Pole and was five hours into his trip when he came in for a landing at Elizabeth's house. He checked his list, gathered the toys that Elizabeth wanted, and was quickly next to her tree placing her presents. He must have made a noise that woke up Elizabeth because as he glanced up, there she stood wide-eyed.

"You're not Santa," said Elizabeth.

"No, I'm Chopper Claus. That's because I ride a chopper motorcycle. You can just call me Uncle," said Chopper. "Santa is my brother and he wants me to deliver presents to this side of the world tonight."

"OK Uncle. Are those my new toys?" she said.

"Yes, they are," said Chopper. "But you should be in bed. You shouldn't see me. It's bad luck. I'll tell you what I'll do. I'll give you one toy to play with right now but then you have to go back to bed. Let's open this gift. It's a peg puzzle."

Elizabeth opened it and knew in an instant that it was much more than a puzzle. It could be a fun game that she could play with her Uncle Chopper.

The puzzle was a wooden board with cutouts. Each cutout contained a puzzle piece that was a form of transportation such as a train, bus, car, plane, or boat. Each piece had a red tab on it so the piece could be lifted out of the cutout. It was a great game for little kids from two to five, but it was a bit too simple for Elizabeth. The idea was to dump out the nine pieces and then pick them up and fit them into the correct openings. On the bottom of each cutout on the board was the same picture that was on the piece. All you had to do was match up the pictures and slip the piece into the opening so it would fit.

"Uncle, I've got a better idea," said Elizabeth. "Let's turn the puzzle into a game that you and I can play together."

"I don't have much time to play a game," said Chopper. "I need to get the rest of the gifts delivered and then ride back to the North Pole. I have a motorcycle ride planned for tomorrow on my motorcycle chopper that the elves gave me last year."

"Oh, pretty please Uncle," cried Elizabeth. "It'll only take a few minutes and it will help me to get sleepy so I can go back to bed like you said. It's a fun game. I just thought it up. You'll like it Uncle."

"All right but we're only going to play it once. OK?" said Chopper.

"Five minutes is all it'll take," said Elizabeth. "This is how we'll play the game. You hide your eyes. Then I'll take the board and remove each piece and place it in plain sight somewhere in either the living room or the hallway. When I have them all placed, I'll tell you. Now, DON'T PEEK."

Little seven-year-old Elizabeth hurried about the two rooms looking for places to put the puzzle pieces. She tried to put most of them on or near her Nana's Santa collection or other Christmas decorations. The first piece went in the whiskers of a tall Santa that stood next to the chair.

She ran back to Chopper and handed him the empty board. "You go find all the pieces and place them in the puzzle board," she whispered in his ear. "I'll help you and tell you when you're hot or cold."

The game was on!

Chopper Claus walked through the hallway and turned right into the living room. "Am I hot or cold," he said.

"You're hot, hot, hot," said Elizabeth. Just then Chopper walked right past one piece and kept walking ahead. "Now you're cold," she said. "But now you're getting warmer, warmer, warmer, hot, hot."

He then went past the sofa and looked over at the end table where there was a group of Santa figures. "Hmmm, let's see here. This Santa has a cart with a polar bear sticking out and ... what's this? There's the boat. I found the first piece," he said. Chopper picked up the piece and placed it in the puzzle.

"There's still a lot of pieces to find," said Elizabeth. "Keep looking."

He still had to find eight more pieces. The light was a little dim in the room, and he looked more intently around the room. He crossed toward a large animated figure of Santa riding a polar bear. It was right next to an antique chair that had been placed next to the Christmas tree.

"I see one," said Chopper. "It's the tow truck right here between Santa's hands. That's number two. I'll place it in the puzzle board. This game is fun, Elizabeth. I still have seven more pieces to go."

To the right of the Santa that was riding a polar bear, was a table next to the window that had a grouping of Santas. They were all Santas based on his own likeness. He had brought these figures on previous Christmases. They depicted many of his own activities with his motorcycles. He peered down and saw a Santa sitting in a sidecar. The attached motorcycle had a puzzle piece laid across the handlebars. It was the police car.

"Ho Ho Ho," said Chopper Claus. "I found the third piece."

"It's taking me too long," said Chopper Claus. "I need more help to find the rest of the pieces."

"Well, you're pretty warm now to find the next piece," said Elizabeth. "How many more pieces do you need?"

"I just put the third piece in the puzzle. There are six more pieces to go," replied Chopper.

Chopper Claus walked to the end of the room, getting hotter and hotter according to Elizabeth.

"You're burning up on fire," she said.

Just then Chopper spied the fourth piece. "I see it on the other sidecar rig," he said. "It's the taxicab."

Chopper placed it in the puzzle and said, "Elizabeth, help me out, please. Where should I look next?"

"I'll give you a big hint," said Elizabeth. "It's clear at the other end of the living room."

Chopper Claus spun around and headed in the other direction. His eyes were darting left and right and up and down looking for another puzzle piece.

"That looks like me sitting in my big chair on top of that writing desk," said Chopper Claus. "I'm holding a fire truck. That's the fifth piece."

"Now if you turn around, you'll be getting hot to find the first piece I hid," said Elizabeth.

Elizabeth was right. As Chopper laid the fifth piece in the puzzle, he turned left and saw the three-foot-high Santa figure holding a Christmas tree in his hands. The helicopter piece had been slipped into his beard.

"I see the helicopter," he said. "Nice job of concealing it in my white beard. That's the sixth piece, and I only have three more to go to complete the puzzle."

"To save you some time Uncle, I'm going to give you another hint," said Elizabeth. "The last three pieces are all in the hallway."

"Well, that should be easy," said Chopper. "Not much out here."

He saw a display on the floor. It looked like his own sleigh with him sitting in it. He was holding a giant candy cane. There were four elves in the sleigh, two in his seat and two at the front of the sleigh. Two polar bears were in front of the sleigh, and the entire display was on a bed of snowflakes.

"What's that down under the seat on top of my right leg?" said Chopper. "It's a puzzle piece, the train. That's the seventh piece of the puzzle."

"The next piece is behind you Uncle," said Elizabeth. "I hid it pretty good and in plain sight."

"Hmmm, lots of stuff out here in the hallway that could conceal the piece," said Chopper. "Nice collection of wooden figures next to the front door. I remember bringing your Nana a few over the years. Wait. That looks out of place. It *is* out of place. There's an ambulance piece up there on the shelf. That's the eighth piece. My puzzle board only has one more piece to go. Got any more hints Elizabeth?"

"Uncle, what do you fill on the fireplace mantle?"

Chopper Claus kept thinking that he needed to finish the game so he could get back to his journey to bring presents to all the children of the world. He knew that when he finished delivering all the toys, it would be time to go for a ride on his chopper motorcycle that had been specially made for him last year. He sure liked that bike.

He wished that everyone could see him on it and see how much he enjoyed riding it.

As he passed the hall stand, he saw a green Jets Football Christmas stocking hanging on a hook. Sticking out of the stocking was the ninth puzzle piece, a school bus.

"I found the last piece Elizabeth," he said. "Thanks for the hint."

"It looks just like the bus I take to go to school," said Elizabeth. "I sure had fun hiding all the pieces and watching you try to find them."

"Ho Ho Ho," said Chopper Claus. "I had lots of fun myself and I'm sorry I won't be able to stay and hide all the pieces so you can play. I need to get back in my sleigh, and you need to get back in your bed and wait for Christmas morning. But, I think I have an idea for next year's toys. I'm going to make a slight change in the puzzle board to make the game even more fun."

"Goodnight Uncle Chopper," said Elizabeth. "I'm very sleepy. I hope you'll bring me your new puzzle game next year. Then we can both take a turn playing it on Christmas Eve."

As Chopper Claus sped through the sky delivering the rest of the toys, he thought about the change he wanted to make to the puzzle board. He wanted one more piece in the puzzle, and he wanted to turn the puzzle board into a puzzle game.

"I like my new chopper motorcycle so much, and I want every boy or girl who plays this new game to think of me," thought Chopper Claus. "I need to make a new piece that shows me on my chopper motorcycle. That way, each child will see me and think to be good all year long each time they play the game."

When Chopper Claus returned to the North Pole and mentioned the idea to the chief elf, the elf went to his workshop and made up a sample puzzle piece. It was a little rough around the edges, but it was just what Chopper Claus wanted.

"Last year, the elves gave me a present, my own motorcycle chopper," said Chopper Claus. "Next year I'll be giving the children of the world a new game and it will include me riding on that same chopper."

"I can't wait to see the expression on Elizabeth's face next year when I give her my new game," said Chopper. "I'll just have to make a little extra noise at her house so she'll wake up again. Then we can play the game she invented, together."

This story was inspired by another Elizabeth—Caroline Elizabeth—whose seven-year-old imagination took an old puzzle and transformed it into a fun game for her Poppy and Nana.

—Walter F. Kern

27. "Sturgis?" "Sturgis!"

I had wanted to go for seventeen years. So it was a pretty big event when I got the vacation I needed and started the planning. It was an even bigger event the morning I was to depart when I woke and started strapping small waterproof duffel bags across the bike's fender. I was on my way—almost.

The sky was incredibly grey, filled with clouds threatening to unleash a torrential downpour. I continued packing with frequent breaks to dubiously scan the sky. I wasted three hours checking weather reports, somehow believing that if I checked enough, the reports would get tired and change. So I got a late start, but was finally headed south down I-81 to meet up with I-80W and take that out to Chicago, where I would meet I-90W and follow it to Sturgis.

81 is one of my favorite interstates. I've trekked down its path on my little red Sportster more times than I can count. I know where the foggy patches are through the mountains of southern Pennsylvania; love the West Virginia rest stops and have felt that bone wearying fatigue that sets in somewhere through Virginia.

80 across Ohio becomes a tedious turnpike but redeemed itself because it was there that the first sightings occurred. I'd pull into a gas station and see a trailer loaded with motorcycles with the driver pumping gas into the accompanying truck. He would be wearing a black shirt with the invariable motorcycle words or graphic on the front. The call and response social dance began:

"Sturgis?" he would say.

And I would respond, "Sturgis!"

And so it began.

Going to Sturgis on a bike is unlike any experience I've ever had, and I've been riding bikes to music festivals and motorcycle events for years. There's always the anticipation, the list making, the packing, then the final launch out of the driveway and on the way to the event. There's the getting close and seeing everyone else who is obviously, by way of clothing and transport mode, going where you are going. There are the greetings, and there are the gas stops where everyone talks to everyone else, finding out where people are from and how long they've been on the road.

All of that is familiar. But I was not prepared for the sheer size of the migration of motorcycles on I-90 headed west or the quick associations among people who had never met before, all bonded by a shared destination. We were so separated from the rest of the people traveling on the interstate, as if the stream of bikes moving toward Sturgis was carried on a river of some reality we had nothing to do with. Other people looked at us and tried to figure out just why they were seeing so many motorcycles that day. We had to continually say "Sturgis!" when they asked, knowing that they did not comprehend the biker mass migration (like salmon), en masse, up the interstates.

After Ohio, I took I-90W through Indiana. 90 becomes a turnpike in Indiana, and—intending no disrespect to Indiana—the only good thing I can say about the Indiana Turnpike is that it is short. The Turnpike is in truly horrible shape. The buildings at the service stations appear to have been built in the 1950s, with low ceilings. A vague I'm-just-waiting-to-be-mugged feeling accompanies a person walking through them. It felt like the slum of the toll roads.

I arrived in Illinois after the short, ugly, stint that was Indiana. And I had thought Indiana was bad. Illinois was a great big toll road, with tons of traffic and a huge nightmare to kick it off called Chicago. I had been making good time up until Indiana, when my stamina started to fade a little bit. I was making perhaps my fifth attempt at the coveted Iron Butt patch.

I desperately want to join the Iron Butt Association. To join it, a person has to ride at least one thousand miles in twenty-four hours and provide documentation of the event. I have tried the Iron Butt run going to Florida, but got lost in South Carolina, where I ended up meeting some South Carolina bikers and having a whole set of unexpected adventures. I was going to try another time after a trip to New York City to see the Dead at Jones Beach, but three days of partying with Long Island bikers kicked my scooter butt. I ended up riding home in the tail end of a hurricane (no joke!) through a hailstorm for part of it and then sleeping on the couch for two days straight. This time I was determined to make it.

But then I met two bikers from Pennsylvania and after we had done the obligatory traveling to Sturgis social dance: "Sturgis?" "Sturgis!" and they had introduced themselves as Chris and Chris, I ended up socializing too long. They had pressed for all of us to go take a 2-hour nap on a picnic table at a rest stop. I kept iterating that I would miss out on my much vaunted goal of making the Iron Butt and this time it was in my sights. They told me it was still doable—even with a nap—if I just rode along with them. It was a big mistake on my part.

We started getting ourselves together after a two-hour snooze. We slept from about five in the morning until seven, when it may have been too cold to ride. As the day started warming up, we drank coffee and stood around our motorcycles, talking. They were convinced we could blast at 90 down the road. I explained to them that mine was an old Sportster, and it had done many miles and one of the ways it's done so many was not to go over 75. It was a chain-drive little beast and the last year of the 4-speed Sporty transmission, to boot. I compensated by running a 22-tooth front sprocket instead of 21, but I'm well aware that my bike was working harder than the big twins I rode next to on the highway to maintain the same speeds. Besides, I didn't like the bone-shaking voyage that consistent 85 miles an hour brings on a chain drive bike.

By the time we got going again, Chris and Chris had decided to put me in the dust. I purposely held back, because I did not like the speed and because I was getting a weird feeling from one of the Chrises. I prefer riding alone most of the time, and was beginning to realize that I would prefer to continue adventuring by myself this time, as well. I was becoming part of a little mini-group's plans instead of my own.

They disappeared at speeds that I'm pretty sure matched the speed of sound. I continued along behind, calculating how many miles I had to do and whether I would make the much vaunted Iron Butt requirements. It was still within my sight. But then I hit Chicago and somehow ended up on the I-90W local headed through the city, rather than the express. The express had a toll booth and plaza at the eastern side of the city and another one at the western side. The local had the same two gas stations and a bevy of toll booths at an approximate distance of one-half mile from each other all through the city. It was maddening.

I was hot. The clouds had long since given way to a blistering heat that radiated off the road. I was doing the old shut-my-engine-off-to-let-my-bike-cool-down-during-the-interminable-standing-waits-at-the-toll-booths routine and pushing it ahead when the traffic was moving. I was becoming increasingly worried about running out of gas. Every toll booth person I asked gave frighteningly complicated instructions about gas stations, and it was becoming obvious that Chicago had—apparently—some anti-terrorist plan to make all its gas stations completely inaccessible. I crept along from tollbooth to tollbooth, seething, swearing to myself, feeling trickles of sweat work their way down my neck and back. I was missing Indiana.

At long last, the madness was over, and I emerged on the other side of Chicago. I stopped at a gas station with a feeling of relief akin to an old style ship pulling into a harbor after weeks at sea. I filled up with gas and then sat on a curb looking at my watch and realizing I had to kiss the Iron Butt dream goodbye—again.

Then, the Pennsylvania bikers pulled into the same gas station, amazed they had found me again with all of us trying to figure out how I had ended up ahead of them. The weird vibe was increasing. One of them got way too close to me. I usually like to keep a distance until I know someone, and he kept grabbing me, suggesting I rub my "titties" up against him. OK, it was time to move on. I was beginning to not like this. He wasn't listening when I said I didn't like it, and he kept on saying he wanted me to take his cell phone number. He suggested we all share a hotel room that night.

"Have you ever done two?" he said.

"Two what?" I asked him, not sure if my impression was the real deal. I did not want to do two. I like sex well enough if it's a person I want to be with, but neither of the Pennsylvania riders qualified. However, I did agree to take their number, enter it into my cell phone, and promise to call that night.

I continued on past Illinois, entering Wisconsin. By then, I was operating on autopilot. I had been too excited to sleep much the night before and had been awake now for too many hours. I pulled into a rest stop in Wisconsin, seeing bikers stretched out on the grassy lawn snoozing or just relaxing. It looked like a good idea and after deleting the Pennsylvania guys' number from my cell phone's memory, I spent a few hours sleeping under a tree through the hottest part of the blazing day.

I got going again in the early evening, doing a run through the dusk to Minnesota, which is where I met Al.

I had pulled into a Minnesota gas station. At the next gas pump over was an old, green Harley Tour Glide. I looked it over and did the social dance with its rider:

"Sturgis?"

"Sturgis!"

The Tour Glide was the same year as my Sporty so its owner, Al, and I had a brief conversation. Al was from Wisconsin. Like me, he preferred to ride about 75. We decided to ride together. He became my angel from Wisconsin.

We had covered most of Minnesota before the temperature started dropping precipitously, and both of us were soon wearing all the riding gear we had brought. We were still cold. Al suggested we find a hotel room, and though I would have liked to continue on, the Iron Butt was a distant dream and the reality of exhaustion and cold was a close presence. A hotel would be good, I agreed.

We ended up at a rinky-dink hotel somewhere in west Minnesota and got the second to last room. The entire hotel was filled with bikers. Al and I stood outside and socialized for a while. I was dead on my feet, however, and the bed beckoned. I went in and lay down while Al stayed and talked to some other Wisconsin bikers. I fell asleep to the sound of Midwestern cadences discussing motorcycle riding. I woke Sunday morning and went outside to tighten my bike's chain. Al came out of the hotel room, and we made our plan for the day: Sturgis or bust! After a quick stop for coffee, we settled into our seats for the last push on the journey.

As we crossed into South Dakota, the surroundings changed from convenience stores called "Whoa and Go" to barren western landscape that surrounded us—everything was West.

We began seeing the interminable signs for Wall Drug Store, and I remembered hearing bikers talk about the ice water and coffee there. Every exit we passed was closer to Sturgis, and I was so incredibly proud of my motorcycle for making it to South Dakota. It's a battered old beast, and I love its heart, its tenacity. Three hundred miles blew by in excessive heat so bad we would drink ice water at each gas stop, drench ourselves from hoses, and be bone dry and thirsty ten minutes later.

80 miles from Sturgis we saw The Storm. It looked eerily biblical. Heavy clouds hung ominously filled with lightning bolts that did a nonstop electrical dance. It was about forty miles dead ahead. Before I went to Sturgis, I talked to many people who had much advice. Some advice was good, and some people had no idea what they were talking about. Many people told me about the wind.

"Oh, watch out for the Western winds," they told me. "They'll blow you clear over into the next lane."

"Yeah, right," I'd say.

I had ridden over 1700 miles so far on this trip, and the wind hadn't been bad. I thought the stories of the western winds were the kinds of things made larger by distance and myth. Then the wind started.

I was noticing a definite cross wind coming directly from my right. I focused ahead on the storm, aware there was no way but through it and dreading every moment. The cross wind built in strength, and I leaned into it, fighting as if an invisible force was pushing my bike inexorably to the left and indeed, that's exactly what was happening. I leaned and got pushed, and leaned and got pushed, and I got progressively more frightened as I realized I was at a severe angle on a straightaway. Then the wind really did push me into the other lane, and that was enough.

I pulled over, almost hyperventilating. It was a frightening experience to be pushed into another lane of traffic—one I would rather not repeat. Those Western winds, they will push you into the other lane. Believe it! Al pulled up behind me and in a gulping voice I told him I simply could not ride anymore. That those winds were too much for me, and there was an increasing chance I would end up road pizza if I continued. As I was talking to Al, other bikers were pulling over all along the side of I-90. Cars and campers began to follow suit. I stood by my bike, putting on my rain gear as the first drops began to come down, watching everything becoming horizontal due to the sheer force of the wind. I was hungry. I was tired. I wanted desperately to get off the road and crawl into a dry, safe tent in a campground.

After what seemed days but was probably only an hour at the most, vehicles began moving again and Al, in his Wisconsin accent, said that it was time for us to be heading toward Sturgis once again. I told Al I would do the best I could, but the wind was still fairly strong, the rain was steady, and I could only go as fast as my Sporty could safely travel under the circumstances. Surprisingly, he said he'd still ride with me—even at my projected turtle's pace—and offered to ride behind with his hazard lights blinking.

It continued raining off-and-on, but the wind abated somewhat. Everything was becoming oversized and otherworldly gigantic. From the massive billboards suspended on huge poles, to the overwhelming numbers of bikers traveling west on the interstate: Motorcycles trailered, motorcycles inside huge campers with tiny garages in the back, and motorcycles ridden by people sharing an experience of solitude in the thousands. Al peeled off the interstate to get to his campground at Exit 32, as I continued on to Sturgis, Exit 30. My angel had left me to fend for myself.

I had daydreamed about Sturgis for years. I had sat in my driveway the first night I brought my bike home daydreaming about eventually riding it to Sturgis. I had a vision of myself entering Sturgis in sunshine, bikers on each side of the road cheering me on and my reliable little bike carrying me, triumphantly, into a golden city called Sturgis where I would be the coolest biker on the planet. I did not live the daydream.

I entered Sturgis a creeping, frightened little mouse, head down, low over handlebars, trying to avoid rain and wind, and miserably overheating in my rain gear. I was tired. I was sore. I was hungry. I was still freaked out by the wind. I was having anxious thoughts about wind being a steady state out west and trying to decide if I had ridden all those miles on a fool's errand, to a place I could not ride without being blown over.

I had completed 1850 miles and was now looking at the biggest traffic jam I had ever seen. My instructions to the campground took me through the town—which I could not simply scoot around the edge of—through the jam of motorcycles that were everywhere around me. I had no choice.

I sat on Lazelle Street in Sturgis for hours as my engine got hotter and hotter. The parade of motorcycles and campers moved so slowly that once again I resorted to the tried and true shut-it-down-and-push-along-when-I-can means of surviving traffic jams with an air-cooled engine. I had a rapidly developing headache, possibly brought on by dehydration, although I didn't realize it at the time.

Eventually, after hours of creep, creep, creep and people hooting and hollering and talking to people while we waited in traffic and going and stopping and going again, I finally got past the Full Throttle Saloon at the edge of town. I took a left onto 79 and found the Iron Horse Campground a few miles down on the right. I pulled in about 10 o'clock at night, weary bodied and bleary eyed, got registration paperwork quickly taken care of, and headed out into the campground in the darkness looking for a flat place to camp. I was too tired to even set up my tent. I just threw down a tarp, then my sleeping bag, and finally another tarp on top. I make this sleeping bag sandwich if I know it's just a quick one night stay when I'm traveling. I made it at Sturgis when I just didn't give a crap.

Monday evening, our little neighborhood of tents decided to take a group trip to Devils Tower, and I went with them. We took a route away from Sturgis and avoided interstates. Devils Tower from a distance looks like a bizarre geographic structure that was picked up from one area of the country and absentmindedly plonked down in the middle of Wyoming.

We finished up the day by riding around Wyoming, getting lost somewhere near Aladdin (population 15) and eventually finding I-90 and taking that back toward Sturgis and the campground.

Sturgis is everything every story has ever said. It is huge; it is loud; it is pure motorcycles for miles. It is a gigantic convention center full of motorcycle things for sale, and it is small operations in booths made of tarps set up alongside the street. It is people wandering, attired in all manner of biker garb, and drunken freaks wandering the sidewalks, shouting "Hello" to all who would listen. It is a parade of motorcycles, any bike one could imagine on two or three wheels: All looks, colors, heights, purposes and piloted by just as differing a group of bikers with beards, no beards, tall, short, wide, Indian, Italian, Harley riders of every sort riding every kind of Harley imaginable. It is a madcap fantasy tale. Bikers have taken over the town, and it has become a biker utopia. It is the loudest, most amazing motorcycle event I have ever witnessed.

I stood on Lazelle Street and felt the air vibrate from the motorcycle engines. It was incredible. I explored Lazelle from one end to the other, meeting people and looking at bikes on the street. License plates heralded riders from every state in the union. In the evening, I went to the Full Throttle Saloon to hear the Reverend Horton Heat, a musician I'd heard great things about. The wind had been picking up during the day, and I was glad I had not been on the road. Another South Dakota storm was rolling in, and everything was blowing sideways.

After a few hours, when the Reverend Horton Heat still had not come on due to the storm and the wind had not abated, I decided it was time to head home. I went outside to where the bus stop was for the little shuttle. I waited in the rain, utterly drunkenly delighted with being in South Dakota. I was completely, happily dry under a rain poncho over my shorts and shirt, even with water running across the toes of my sandal clad feet. I wasn't exactly positive I was waiting in the right place. I usually navigate by landmarks and nothing seemed the same as it had many hours ago, when the world was dry and light. So after a while, when a little van pulled in, with "Da Cab" painted in large letters across the side, I was thrilled that I had done something right in my inebriated state. The company that ran the shuttle bus—called "Da Bus"— also ran a taxi service called "Da Cab" during Bike Week. I went over to the van and asked if they knew where the stop for Da Bus was.

The bus driver said, "As of now, Da Cab IS Da Bus. Get in."

The van took me out to the Buffalo Chip Campground, just as one of their big concerts was letting out.

The traffic was crazy. Motorcycles were all over the road in the driving rain, with four wheel vehicles surrounded by smaller vehicles, and everyone everywhere. At least one bike had gone down in the mud, and the bus driver had her head stuck out the window, trying to see through the weather and yelling at all of the bikers to get out of the way.

We eventually nosed our way through the traffic, back out onto a side road, and eventually to my campground where the van took me right to my tent and dropped me off. I shucked off my rain gear, crawled inside, and went gratefully to sleep for the night.

Thursday our campground neighborhood took a collective ride to Custer State Park. I was invited to be a passenger for the day. Usually I like the independence of riding my own bike but after some consideration of benefits to occasional passengerdom, I decided to take advantage, mixed up some vodka and ice tea, and boarded a back seat of a yellow Gold Wing. I hesitate to include this section, which includes the image of me, upon the back seat of the aforementioned Gold Wing, guzzling my ice tea and vodka concoction, shouting lustily at anything and anyone we went by, and naming my ride "The Taxi" due to its bright yellow tint. To those who know me, riding on a Honda is an unexpected detour from my normal modes. I am firmly a Harley rider. However (and here goes my frantic attempt at justification), I believe that life is experienced best when someone does what is not expected.

I can now say, based on experience, that I love Harleys best. I'm not saying that the Gold Wing was a bad bike, for it was not. It was a seamless machine which glided through curves and took us past Rushmore and on through Custer Park. It was an excellent machine, and I took full advantage of the cup holders and arm rests and speakers and wind flange things. It's just that it had no thunder. When I ride my motorcycle, there is a dialog between the two of us. I listen to its engine, and I feel the way it handles. It tells me how the road is, and I tell it which one to travel on. I once got to ride a friend of mine's old Super Glide, and as I rode, it tried to have a conversation with me. I heard its engine thunder the way it does for its owner. I felt the frame telling me about the road. The transmission gave me a conversational greeting every time I shifted. A Gold Wing, while an eminently competent bike, does none of these things. It simply goes. There is no soul; there is no conversation. I ride a bike for adventure and companionship. So I guess I'll stick with my Sportster.

We took a back road to I-90 that led toward Rapid City and on to Custer Park. One of the park's claims to fame, along with amazing views and over seventy thousand acres of land, is the buffalo herd. We were looking forward to seeing the herd thunder across the road in front of us. Every time we stopped, we asked if a herd was nearby. And each time we were told how it had just passed through, or was only a little ways ahead of us. We saw no buffalo.

Saturday, I started packing up to head home. After a morning of puttering and preparing for a quick exit Sunday morning, I went into Sturgis one last time. I hitchhiked again, not wanting to ride in the molasses of the town. After wandering thoroughly up and down Lazelle Street, I took a cross-street and made an amazing discovery: Lazelle Street was not the main thoroughfare! In fact, it was just a side show.

All week long, I had thought I was at the center of Sturgis when I was merely at the warm up. I still am not sure exactly how I managed to miss this great truth. However, having newly discovered the center of Sturgis Bike Week to be Main Street, I resolved to spend the day exploring all that I had missed. I wandered up and down, talking and socializing to the point of exhaustion in the August heat.

Sunday morning I wanted to get up and go. I had prepared for a quick exit and mostly, it was that, except for one long, extended shower. When I'm on the road, showers aren't a frequent occurrence, and I wanted to start out clean.

I rode like a banshee East on I-90, passed Pioneer Auto and the Mitchell Corn Palace without even a second thought of stopping to check them out. I made it over 400 miles with a few brief stops for gas and short conversation before getting into Minnesota where I stopped again for gas. And then my bike wouldn't start.

Each time I hit the starter, I heard a circuit breaker sounding like it was tripping and resetting—a clicking sound coming from under my seat. I swore softly to myself as I wheeled away from the gas pumps and settled down at the side of the gas station to consult my service manual to try to fix the problem.

A gaggle of Minnesota bikers came over, asking if I needed help. I explained my situation, and everyone gave their opinions as to what could be wrong. I ended up atop my ride, with a biker on each side of me and one behind. They pushed my bike for all they were worth, and I tried to start it by popping the clutch. That didn't work. The clicking noises persisted, and I was prepared to start checking circuit breakers.

One guy asked, "What's the last thing you did to your bike?" I told him about replacing the turn signal flasher after arriving in Sturgis. It had given out sometime on I-90W between Illinois and South Dakota. Based on that, we took a look behind the headlight and— lo and behold!—the problem was a short circuit. My panic abated.

The Minnesota bikers sent me on my way, after giving me a phone number to call when I got home so they would know I made it. After a few more hours in the saddle, I pulled into a campground, set up my sleeping bag sandwich and went to sleep for the night.

Monday morning, I woke up bound and determined to make it to Pennsylvania. I headed through Minnesota at a furious clip, barely stopping for gas, which was—it turned out—a mistake.

Once again, I had made a faulty estimation and ended up coasting up an exit ramp, with reserve fuel gone and the bike in neutral. A Minnesotan on a bicycle came over and offered to help me push the last few yards into the gas station. Gassed up, I continued on through the last of Minnesota, crossed the spectacular Mississippi River, and entered Wisconsin.

By Monday night, I had made it to Indiana. I finally had to stop when exhaustion became an unwanted passenger on my trip. I prefer camping in a tent next to my bike over any other accommodations on the road. I like the feeling of partnership that develops when I tie a tarp to my bike's handlebar and sleep under it, after checking oil and chain tension. A I-take-care-of-the-bike-and-it-takes-care-of-me sensibility develops on a long trip. There was nothing I liked at this exit, so I moved on.

I got off at the next exit, hoping to find a small campground. I was willing to stay at whatever came up first. I saw a hotel advertising $29.95 per night. The parking lot was filled with motorcycles. This would be my resting place for the evening. I pulled in, requested a room on the ground floor and was told they had none left. I got a second floor room, and after parking down below, unloaded the few items I would need for the night, and headed to my room. My head hit the pillow, and I remembered nothing until dawn.

In the morning, I went downstairs to tighten my chain and check my bike over before the day's ride. I had noticed oil coming from under one of my tappet blocks, and had been nervously watching it all the previous day, hoping it wouldn't speed up or turn into an oil explosion as a gasket gave way completely. Throughout the day I was checking the tappet block, trying to decide if it was a slow leak or a fast seep, and beginning a fervent prayer that I make it home without a problem.

My old bike had been through a relentless, pounding voyage, and the pace was taking a toll. I had lost a bolt at the bottom of my rear exhaust pipe somewhere on my journey, and had stuck a piece of scavenged safety wire into the hole, twisting it as tightly as I could and hoping it would do the job at preventing vibration. I was proceeding on fervent hope and luck as my bike and I rattled and rolled our way across the Eastern United States.

Every time I stopped, I checked my bike over—hoping nothing else had given way or was leaking—and took a break from the unending vibrations from the bike.

My ride had been slowed down considerably by my frequent checks and prayers. I entered Pennsylvania sometime in the early afternoon, happy to be one state from home. I had a plan worked out in my mind that involved renting a truck if the worst happened and my bike could not continue.

The leak continued its relaxed rate, and I continued my agitated checking on it, convinced I heard noises I didn't usually hear and hoping I was wrong.

I rode along I-80 as fast as my rattling little bike dared to go, enjoying the views where the highway cuts through the mountains and reliving scenes from Sturgis in my mind. I was the biker running solo across the landscape, giggling to myself as I remembered various things that had happened fifteen hundred miles earlier. I passed the time looking for buffalo, figuring my chances were about as good in Pennsylvania as they'd been in South Dakota. The ride became less funny as evening came in and decidedly serious as the fog settled in behind the darkness. I was in the Pennsylvania Mountains, barely able to see two car lengths ahead of me, with great, big trucks barreling along as fast as their governors allowed. Then the road construction started.

The highway narrowed to one lane going in either direction, with concrete barricades dictating lane access as we approached bridge construction. One of the giant trucks was trying to get into the lane its driver wanted and cut around the car ahead of me. The truck zinged back into place as the lanes narrowed, and its trailer hit one of the barricades. Little bits of yellow plastic lens reflectors tore off and scattered amidst the traffic in a brilliant show. He barely slowed down, and I wondered how things would be if it had been my little taillight he had tried zinging around, instead of the car ahead.

A rest stop came along, and I got off the highway, relieved to have a break. The rest stop was calm and still. I enjoyed the peace after the frenetic movement of the highway. I enjoyed the fact that all the big trucks parked there were not moving, and there were no small pieces of flying plastic to dodge. I sat at a picnic table, took out a map and figured out how many hundreds of miles I had to go. Home was getting closer.

I followed I-80 to Scranton, where it intersected with I-81, which I took north toward home. I arrived back at my trailer tired, dirty, battered and spent. My body was sore from the relentless shaking, and my bike looked as if it had completed a cross country trip in four days, which, in retrospect, it had. I unloaded two weeks of dirty laundry and threw it in the washer, spread out my tent to dry on the lawn, and sat down by my Sportster to survey the damage.

My bike had bled its heart out through a gasket, had a warped exhaust pipe from the relentless vibrating after the bolt had gone, and had South Dakota dust still wedged in various crevices. It was almost as badly damaged as it was after my trip to Tennessee. But that's another story...

—Yonah Luecken

28. Beet, a Diehard Biker

One thing about being a biker for many years is that you see, hear, and do things most motorcyclists don't.

Quite a number of years ago, an acquaintance got hurt in an accident on his bike. He went by the name of Beet, and he was as hard-core and as dirty a SOB as they came. I saw him once in a juke-joint, and he had casts on his left leg and right arm. He also had stitches on his face and many bruises. Some club brothers were putting his Harley Knucklehead (Knuck) back on the road for him.

A few weeks later, I was at a biker event talking with friends, and someone started shouting, "Beet's here. He's coming in." The group parted, and in rode Beet on his Knuck.

Naturally, Knucks are jock-shifted and suicide-clutched—the only way to ride. Several guys grabbed him as he stopped so he would not fall over.

How did he ride in his condition? Easy! First, they tied his left foot to the clutch pedal. Then, they looped a rope around his knee and tied it to the gas tank. Finally, they fastened his hand to the throttle with black electrical tape. His right leg was OK.

He was a tough diehard ole SOB for sure. He died of old age.

—Edeee2

29. Afghanistan by Motorbike - The Dead Body

It was five in the morning in the little Asian town of Herat, which lies just inside Afghanistan on the western border with Iran. It was the dawning of a clear day, and I was itching to get out on the road.

My Norton 750cc Commando motorcycle, nicknamed "Demeter" (after the Greek Goddess of Life) stood in the morning sunlight ready to roll out into the Afghan Desert.

She had already carried me from England, through France, Monaco, Italy, Austria, Yugoslavia, Greece, Turkey, and Iran. But there was somehow a mystery about today's trip: 400 miles through a pure desert on a concrete road built by the Russians.

I had been advised to go in a convoy through this stretch en route through Helmund Province to Kandahar, but I was in no mood to wait for other travellers to rally together. I was used to being on my own now. I kick-started the bike, feeling a fresh excitement.

Demeter and I purred out of town into the wilderness. The feeling of "freedom" was overwhelming. The desert sun was warm and welcoming, and I decided to pull over and redress for the occasion. I took off my shirt and shoes, and set off again wearing only a pair of shorts and a big set of headphones atop my mop of crispy hair.

George Harrison's album, "All Things Must Pass," rang out as I pressed the button on the cassette player neatly strapped on top of my canvas bag on the back rack. This was what it was all about, Afghanistan at our fingertips, not a care in the world, with the mystery of the unknown out on the road ahead.

On we strode, Demeter and I, into the desert. Hour after hour we hummed through the desolate, striking beauty of the empty brownness of the desert. Sometimes the road was Romanesque, and as straight as a die, disappearing on the far horizon through a lightly rolling sand-scape. Then it would suddenly change into a craggy rockscape and wind up and down through the low cliffs of jagged rock terraces. Then, without warning, it was back to the straightness of an open space as endless as eternity.

The sun got hotter, and the road ahead shimmered in the haziness and the mirages of water pools, which became an entertaining way to conjure up hallucinations controlled by the mind, but definitively ruled by nature.

My body was by now dark chocolate brown, having followed the summer sun continuously through months of travel. My dressing down to only a pair of shorts was no problem even in the scorching midday Afghan heat, since the breeze of forward motion was soothing, even in the dryness of the hot desert air.

The cassette played on, and I was just settling down to a new track as I came down and out of a rocky crag. There, in front of me, was a "dead" man lying across the roadway.

Another man, evidently distressed, was throwing his hands to the heavens and dancing a lament, rhythmic like a Morris dancers jig, although he had no bells around his ankles. Wait. Hang on a minute, it all seemed rather controlled, and his jig was looking quite professional.

Demeter sprang into their view, and the growling classic sound of the Norton triggered an unexpected reaction. The jigger glanced, pranced, then ran like hell for the edge of the road. Within a split second, the "dead" man was also up and running, and they ran hell-for-leather into the deep desert sand.

Speaking of leather, as Demeter and I cruised past, I noticed the dancing man had a rather large leather camel whip gripped menacingly in his hand. Then the vision struck me; they were a couple of desert-muggers! A "dead man" lying in the road would have stopped many a traveller eager to help in a desperate situation, but on this occasion a large yellow motorcycle swings around the corner and thunders towards them. Having had no previous knowledge of growling two-wheeled machines, they freak out genuinely and run for their lives.

A warm flood of emotion filled my body, and I heard my gasp for air as I realised that I had just flipped through a potential disaster, avoiding the probable end of my dream to travel from England to South Africa on a motorcycle!

I then found myself laughing out loud, rolling the bike from side to side, shaking my head, punching the air with my fist, and then singing along with Demeter and George Harrison, rejoicing at our lucky escape.

I pulled over after another 10 miles and danced my own jig at the side of the road. The feeling of "freedom" was overwhelming, and I cupped my hands and screamed a call of delight and breathed a deep breath and called again. I was alive, and the world was all before me! Then my body shook uncontrollably in retaliation, just as my screeching call echoed back off a craggy rock face, and caught me unawares. The hairs on the back of my head crackled and stood on end. I cringed, and then felt fulfilment. Life was indeed great!

I filled the petrol tank with fuel from the reserve can, checked the luggage straps, and then cast my eye over the bike to ensure all was well. Demeter kick-started first time, and we were off again through the Afghan desert. George Harrison lent us his voice with "Plug Me In." Demeter and I struck out for our destination, the town of Kandahar, lying deep in the southern Afghan desert.

As we motored on, I saw something quite unbelievable on the road ahead, but that is for another story.

—Bruce Curran

Editor's Note: Bruce's book, *Blow Ur Horn*, is available at www.booksondemand.com.ph and contains this story.

30. Afghanistan by Motorbike - The Relativity of Travel

The sun scorched the rock and sand on both sides of the covered road between Herat and Kandahar in the Afghan desert. The motorcycle purred perfectly as my bike and I glided through the emptiness of the open spaces. I had just avoided a near disaster at the hands of two desert-muggers, and was contemplating my luck as something quite amazing appeared on the road ahead.

My eyes were vaguely focused within the haze of the sun's dancing rays. I began to imagine a string of English words in red paint written across the backboard of a cart rolling along ahead of me on this Russian built road. The words continued to prance before me in the heat of the morning sun, and I knew I must be hallucinating. Then clarity was upon me and there on the road were the words: "FIRST WALK AROUND THE WORLD."

My jaw dropped in recognition, and then closed again in realisation, as my mind reminded me of the many flying bugs that are acrid to swallow, especially at high speed! I braked slowly and drew nearer. I could now see two people walking beside a large grayish brown mule hitched to a cart. On the cart lay some rucksacks, and food and straw for man and beast. I drew up alongside, and the group drew to a halt.

"Hello there," I grated, as the desert dust scratched my throat. "You're not serious about that sign on the back of your cart are you?"

"I'm afraid so," spoke a dark figure with a North American accent.

My mouth dropped and closed once more. Then they unravelled their tale before me like a magic carpet.

The two friends had set out from Missouri in the Mid-Central United States, walked to the east coast, then shipped to Portugal where they bought the mule and slung their rucksacks across its back. Eventually, they arrived in Istanbul, Turkey and purchased a cart to carry food and water for the oncoming desert and open country crossings so typical of this part of Asia.

After Turkey, Iran had been crossed and here they were halfway through Afghanistan. They were excited because they were over halfway around the world, with over two and three quarter years under their belt, and only an estimated two and one quarter years to go!

It got me thinking about how relative journeys are to the experience of other people and, in a flash, I realised how important an earlier experience of mine had been in my own travels.

Alec and I had left England on two identical motorcycles many months before, after four years of dreaming and two years of saving. On our third day, some three hours south of Paris, a great tragedy occurred.

Alec was caught in a vicious crosswind that tumbled him off his bike onto the toll road at 70 mph. I watched helplessly from behind as he went into a wave pattern weaving from side to side, which built momentum till he lost control completely. He toppled to his side and skidded with the bike onto the central reservation, before coming to an ugly halt near his revving machine.

His bike's throttle was jammed-on and screamed in agony. But it was mechanical agony, unlike the physical pain that had instantly smothered Alec on the open road.

I noticed what a beautiful sunny afternoon it was that day in France. Eight days later, Alec was on a train back to England, with a rucksack on his back and a hobbling cane to help him support his plastered right leg—not broken, but twisted.

During those eight days, I lived out my life in my little green tent perched in a field near the hospital close to the town of Joigny. My thoughts were mixed and unclear, imprecise and confused, long and short, but most of all quisitive about what I was going to do.

One minute, I had been on a great adventure with my best friend and the next, I was alone and at a major crossroad. Should I go back and drift into the routines of an English lifestyle? Should I tackle the road ahead on my own and continue the planned journey through Europe, Asia and Africa? Perhaps, I could just curl up in a ball and imagine nothing had happened! It was my first real meeting with myself, my first insight into the fickleness of life, and the unknown road that lies before all of us.

The mule snorted violently, and my mind returned to the present and the group before me.

"Gee! The mule's thirsty again?" mused the other North American, taller than his friend, but just as dark from the years on the road. "That's the third time in the last hour he's asked for water!"

As they went about their business, I wished them well and kick-started my bike to continue on my way. I glanced in my rear view mirror one more time, and caught a shimmering image of the group that quickly faded into a mirage of truth that lay before me on the path ahead.

The sun continued to scorch the rocks and sand either side of the covered road between Herat and Kandahar in the Afghan Desert.

—Bruce Curran

Editor's Note: Bruce's book, *Blow Ur Horn*, is available at www.booksondemand.com.ph and contains this story.

31. Jailed in Afghanistan

The Khyber Pass is the traditional route out of Afghanistan into Pakistan east of Kabul, the capital city. But the Bolan Pass is the alternative road in the south of the country running through the river valley winding towards the border to the east of Kandahar, and that was the post I was approaching.

I was conscious of the time, since I had been told that the border post closed at 6 p.m., and it was already past 5:45 when I drew up to the gatepost. Two men in traditional long loose Afghan shirts and trousers explained with hand language that it was too late to cross, and I had to go back. It was well over an hour back to Kandahar, so I explained that I was going to stay there if they did not let me through the gate. They called over someone who spoke some English, and the arrangement was to be that I could stay, but the only bunk bed available was in the border jail behind metal bars. That was fine with me.

They agreed that it would be safe to leave my bike out front fully packed. Then, the creaking iron door was duly opened and clanged shut behind me. I heard the big metal key turning in the lock, and there I was, incarcerated (voluntarily) in Afghanistan.

I had one inmate for company, and, as it turned out, he spoke very good English, and we ended up talking almost all through the night. Here is his story:

He was a Pakistani not too keen on some of the Islamic government outlooks and treatment of non-Moslems in the country. He had decided to get out of the country, and somehow worked out a scheme for getting over to Canada to join his brother who had settled there. Needless to say, he was a non-Moslem himself.

His problem was that the Afghan border authorities had bumped him off the passenger bus crossing into Afghanistan and were going to bundle him back into Pakistan the next day. He was terrified that he would be tortured in Pakistan (as had happened to a few of his compatriots). His situation had occurred at the time of one of the Indo-Pakistan Wars that would later prevent me crossing the border into India. But, for now, my inmate was a very anxious, unhappy man.

We schemed during the night, and before the break of dawn, I was back on my bike heading back to the town of Kandahar. We had decided that the only chance he had was to be declared an Indian citizen, by pleading with the Indian Consul based in Kandahar.

I took with me a photo of him and copies of his signatures, and went out in earnest—much to the surprise of the border personnel—as I turned the bike around, and headed away from their border gate.

I arrived in Kandahar and was soon guided to the right home and knocked on the front wooden door at 8:30 a.m. As it happened, I got him out of his morning bath, but at least he had agreed to see me.

"Good Morning Sir. I understand that you are the Indian Consul here. I have come on behalf of someone who needs your concerted assistance," I said.

The Consul replied, "What help will this good man be needing?" He was, no doubt, mystified by this dust ridden foreigner out on a limb far from home, asking for help for someone else out here in the vast emptiness of Asia.

"He is a Pakistani who needs to be declared an Indian citizen so that he can go to Canada," I volunteered.

"I am not understanding. Please enlighten me," the Consul said, looking somewhat puzzled.

I went through the entire background and rigmarole of this lonely man about to be sent back for possible torture. The Consul agreed that there was a lot of sense to the story, and it was a theme already known to him. He told me that he would keep the photo and signatures, and do what he could.

The fact was that he expected that the authorities would first bring this man to Kandahar for processing before sending him back to Pakistan. In this case, the Consul assured me, that he *would* hear about it and step in to assist him as best he could.

Outside his front door, I kick-started the bike and his final parting words to me were: "I will be looking out and will step in and do the best I can for this friend of yours. Oh, have a safe journey."

In all of this, I sensed the diplomat in him and knew that there would always be a part of bravado in all he said, in efforts to satisfy all who came before him with requests of all colours of the rainbow. But at the same time he did impart "hope" and I set off back to the border post with only words and no documents for my inmate living in suspension, in the jail.

I arrived, was re-jailed, and explained all that had been said and what might happen, provided he was sent back to Kandahar before being bussed back to Pakistan.

What could I do? I bade him farewell, kick-started "Demeter," left him in a vacuum of hope, and set off in search of my own destiny, passing into no-man's land between the two borders.

I realised that I would never know what happened and if my inmate would make it to his "freedom" and across the seas with an Indian passport to be reunited with his brother in Canada.

It felt good but strange to be totally free to go on my way in what direction I chose. I headed for the Pakistani border post and so began the entry formalities for my ninth country since I had left the home shores of England some seven months previously. Unbeknownst to me, this part of the trip would involve *Playboy Magazine*.

The Pakistani border guard was immaculately dressed in his uniform, with a waxed moustache that looked like the proverbial military officer fully in charge of all around him.

"And where, may I ask, have you come from on your motorbike?" he asked inquisitively.

"From England," I answered, still preoccupied with the fate of my inmate, abandoned in Afghanistan.

Then I could not quite believe my ears as the Immigration officer spoke with a softened voice, "I say, you don't happen to have a *Playboy* magazine with you, do you?"

Instantly, I had visions of Islamic women embroiled in burkhas and black dowdy garb, deliberately designed, or so it seems, to dampen any spark of interest in a woman by any man in view. The Immigration officer looked very disappointed when I did not whip out six magazines, all full of gorgeous buxom women, scantily dressed in evocative dowdy garb aimed to send men to the edge of their desires. He faded back into his seat, stamped my passport with a grudging sweep, and wished me well on my continuing journeys.

There was just one rather important fact that he neglected to tell me, no doubt smothered by his own disappointment to be still "Playboy-less" deep within his own society. I had all the way since France driven through eight countries on the right hand side of the road, and never on the left since leaving England. But here I was at the border of a country with a British Colonial past, and, therefore, a different road sense, where everything was in reverse, and driving on the left was the standard.

I mounted "Demeter" and she started first time. I rode off down the road on the right hand side (as per usual) only to see a large passenger bus heading straight toward me. The bus was well crowded, with people even seated outside on the roof of the vehicle. Several people on top started pointing to their right and in my ignorance, thinking them being friendly, was nodding my head to thank them for pointing out the fantastic scenery off to the right hand side of the road. I nodded again, but then as the bus bore down on me, I heard cries of anguish from atop the bus. In an instant, I swung to the left, as I realised within a hair's breadth of disaster, that I was not supposed to be an admiring traveller, but a responsible driver clamped on the left hand side of the roadway.

My heart jumped into my throat. My smile at the passengers was pathetic. Then, my fury at the immigration officer became unbounded. Such is the craving for sexuality! However, I thought better of going back, telling him of my plight, and possibly causing him job loss and another reason to blame "the West" for his predicament.

This tale reminds me of an incident that happened to me in the Philippines some 30 years later:

> I had been delighted to be invited to share the use of the clubhouse of the Mad Dogs Motorcycle Club in Manila. At the time, they had a monthly Club magazine and invited me to write about my motorcycle journeys. I duly obliged, and one weekend was approached by two of the club members. Dressed all in black, with black leather waistcoats sporting the club badge, they were both tattooed on their arms with their bulldog club emblem and club member number. They cornered me in a friendly manner and told me they had

enjoyed my tales to-date but were curious about any sexual encounters I might have had on my journeys. I promised to feed them a tale for the next issue.

I conjured up a tale to be remembered and took a leaf of belief from my good friend, Hugo Wray, who is always reminding us to "never let the truth get in the way of a good story."

The "true" truth was that I had remained entirely celibate throughout my trip in Asia on my bike. But a vision sprang to mind, and I rolled out a tale of going wholeheartedly into a brothel in Kandahar, and dreamt up lucid lines of sexual encounters with two ravenous women and me, a foreigner, in need of fulfilment and satisfaction. If half the story line had been real, I would have been a happy man but the real encounter was with the two Mad Dogs who hailed my achievements at publication, and I became their best of buddies from then on. Such is the craving for sexuality! Ride well guys!

I rode on to Quetta where a keen motorcyclist invited me to his family home for dinner, then on through Sukkur, and finally down into the coastal city of Karachi on the edge of the Arabian Sea that leads into the vastness of the Indian Ocean. On the way, I crossed the mighty Indus river (a magical experience). It flows majestically all the way down from the very north of the country from the mountain range that is the mother of them all, the Himalayas.

The plan had been to ride on into India with its remarkable history, but the onset of yet another Indo-Pakistan War put paid to that idea, since the border crossings were sealed.

I decided to disembark from Asia by booking a passenger ship with the Italian Lloyd Triestino line docking in Karachi and sailing to East Africa. But the wait was to be over six weeks till the next liner. I had also run out of money at a time when the War had somehow messed up money transfer transactions. So, I sat in Karachi with no money to my name.

Asghar Zackria inadvertently came to my rescue. He was a Karachi bike fanatic who tracked me down to my hotel. He invited me to his home for dinner, and the next day introduced me to a group of bikers who met regularly in the evenings. They had only heard about my bike, a Norton Commando 750cc, but had never seen one till "Demeter" rolled into town with all her power and beauty.

The bike became an instant hit with the group, and being a big bike, she was obliged to carry three people on the rides around town. Riding this way was a novelty for me, and I felt a bit like a praying mantis crouched up front guiding the bike with two passengers behind. Here was my instant route to friendship and, as it happened, my rescue from my temporary moneyless state.

The bike group fed me, looked after me, and essentially kept me alive. The hotel bills stacked up, but the money eventually came to put everything back on an even keel. Sardar, their local mechanic, was a genius, and although he had never seen a Commando, he had been brought up with British manufactured bikes, knew how they ticked, and was smart enough to fix one major problem of mine. He traced a disturbing knocking sound to a slightly shifted alternator inside the primary chain case, and after a riveting, it behaved properly again.

Asghar had long admired a Triumph Bonneville that had sat abandoned at the British Embassy for two years. He had dreamed of owning the bike someday. A few months ago, I had waltzed into the Embassy, made the right contact, and got the Australian address of the owner who had left the bike there when the crankshaft snapped. Correspondence by letters and a price-negotiation resulted in Asghar becoming its proud owner. He was now riding that Bonneville, but it needed work. (I found out later—after I arrived in Africa—that Sardar rebuilt the bike and Asghar did a 2000 mile trip around his own country of Pakistan.)

My bike and I were secured aboard the ship and early one evening, we left for East Africa. Asghar, Sardar, Mohammed Hussein, and the rest of the bike gang sat astride their bikes at the end of the dock, and flashed their headlights as the ship pulled out to sea.

It was a very emotional farewell, and I shed a tear or three as Asia and the gang disappeared over the horizon. I recalled their friendship, the weeks together, including a 3-day trip on a 1942 Willy Jeep into the wilds of the Baluchistan desert, a swimming ride on the back of a sea turtle, and the charm that was the city of Karachi.

I slept soundly as the ship rolled away south on a gentle sea. Africa lay before me.

—Bruce Curran

Editor's Note: Bruce's book, *Blow Ur Horn*, is available at www.booksondemand.com.ph and contains this story.

32. I Remember How Scary It Was

About 1967, I found a seriously-taken-apart Harley motorcycle. I loaded it into the trunk of my '55 Chevrolet and took it to my workshop.

I had no idea what I had except that it was an old Harley. I rode Triumphs then.

I separated parts, washed them, chased threads on bolts and nuts, and was ready to try to assemble the parts into a motorcycle.

I went to the local bike shop, asked many questions, and looked for advice. As I talked to the owner, another biker came in the door. The owner pointed to him and said, "That's the guy you need to talk to."

I introduced myself and proceeded to explain my troubles. Unbeknownst to me, he was president of the local one-percenters. We became friends, and he was soon helping me build my first Harley.

He told me it was a 1937 Knucklehead. (He called it a Knuck.) It had a suicide clutch and a jock-shift. We got it going and rode a few short rides together.

My new friend invited me and my girlfriend to go on a weekend run with his club. We were on our way and were stopped at a red light. Suddenly, my girlfriend shifted her weight. I lost my balance, and my foot came off the clutch. The rear tire barked, and we shot through the light. The traffic stopped, and my new friends followed me straight through the red light, right on my tail.

I was the man of the hour. They never knew the truth.

—Triple-e

33. The Biker

I have been riding motorcycles for about 20 years and can only remember a few times that I've run into what I consider to be a hardcore biker. I am not referring to what most people think of as a one-percenter. I am talking more about a person who can work miracles with a pocket knife and a roll of duct tape, a true loner, a unique character with the instincts, imagination, and survival skills to do battle with and prevail against the gremlins that place most of us at the mercy of 800-roadside assistance and the knowledge and expertise of others. I remember one such character in particular.

About 10 years ago, I rode to Bike Week in Daytona, Florida with my friend, Robert, and his girlfriend. She was a cute, petite little thing who rode a blacked out, pumped up Harley Softail Custom. She was good company and fun to ride with, always smiling and never complaining. But, she would not ride more than 400 miles a day. When she hit that mark, the riding was over for the day. However, this story is not about her.

Our 400 mile mark on this trip was Perry, Florida where we checked into a small, cheap motel.

In the parking lot next to my room, was an ancient chopper in pieces spread out all over the place. There was an old, rough looking guy sitting on the ground next to the bike. He and the bike looked like they belonged to each other. He was sifting through parts and appeared to be putting the bike back together.

I spoke to him, and we talked for a little while. He told me he was from Georgia and was on his way to Daytona when his bike broke down in Perry three days earlier. He had built the bike himself, putting it together from scratch using a variety of parts.

The frame was from an old Triumph, and everything else was Heinz 57 or homemade. After breaking down, he took a Greyhound bus from Perry to Tallahassee (about 45 miles away). He spent a couple of days there going to local shops, digging through their dumpsters and trash piles looking for parts and pieces that he thought would work. He had just made it back to Perry earlier that afternoon, and was now in the process of sorting

115

through the various parts, trying to figure out how to put everything back together and make it work.

I would have bet the title on my bike that he would never see Daytona on that thing.

Well, I got up early the next morning, and he and his bike were gone. I can only assume that he got her put together sometime during the night and rode off.

Now to me, he was a hardcore biker.

—Joe2wheels

34. Attack of the U.F.M.

It all started on a sleepy autumn morning. I rode to work early, usually getting up around 4:30-4:40 a.m. and left around 5:00-5:10 a.m. Needless to say, I'm usually only partially awake at that time in the morning.

I donned my leathers and headed out to the garage. I opened the garage door and backed out Mistress, my V-Star 1100 Classic, and got the rest of my gear on: gloves, face mask, clear riding glasses, and half helmet. I tucked my lunch inside my right saddlebag. It was cold enough outside that I had trouble keeping the glasses from fogging up when I breathed out my nose.

I closed the garage door and proceeded to start the bike. I turned the ignition key on all the way. I made sure the choke (fuel enrichment knob) was turned on all the way. Then, I made sure the fuel cut-off valve was turned to the ON position, remembering that if I do not turn the fuel knob back on, I will not make it out of my neighborhood without running out of fuel and stalling the bike. Don't ask me how I know this.

I pressed the cut-off switch to the run position and hit the start button. Mistress' 1100 V-Twin roared to life. With the Cobra exhaust, you can bet my neighbors know when I leave in the morning. I slid the fuel enrichment knob (works like a choke) over to idle the engine down some and headed carefully out of my driveway onto the dark, damp street.

It was a cold, dark, and foggy Monday morning. I turned out of my neighborhood and headed eastbound on Cheek Sparger Road. I straightened out from the turn and started to accelerate. Just then, I caught some movement off the side of the road, just barely visible at the edges of the headlamp pattern.

At first, I didn't pay too much attention to it, thinking it was probably just a rabbit on the side of the road hopping around. Then I noticed that the anomaly was headed perpendicularly to my track on the road and would cross right in front of me. That's when I spotted the glowing, white beady eyes of this creature fixated on Mistress and me, reflected from the lights.

As I got closer, I could make out its size. It was larger than an alley cat and more like the size of a small dog. Now I could make out some large teeth and huge fangs in a pointy snout and large whiskers with foam trailing out the corners of its mouth. Just then, I realized what the Unidentified Flying Marsupial (UFM) was: a very angry opossum running at full gallop across the road and heading straight for me.

It looked like it was out for blood. For all I knew it could be rabid. I raised the angle on my right wrist, and Mistress responded by slowing down some, both of us hoping to throw the attacker's timing off. I knew it was going to either try to get up underneath my front tire and knock me off my bike or jump straight up for a death grip on my throat.

My change-in-speed-to-throw-off-the-timing ploy did not work.

My next tactic was to aim my V-Star 1100 right at it. Mistress nodded in agreement. The logic in this approach was that, if I tried to hit a moving target, more than likely I would fail. The gargantuan opossum was at a full-out run and just fixing to spring at me; its claws glistened in the riding lamps, when its head hit my front tire.

It made a hollow thump-type sound. At this point, neither one of us could adjust the momentum we had built up. The killer slid underneath the path of the bike. I could feel the rear of the bike lift up as the rear tire ran over the marsupial's head. I knew it was its head because if it had been its body, the back end of the motorcycle would have bounced up a lot higher.

In a flash, it was over. Mistress and I had thwarted a deadly attack from a killer opossum and barely survived. I tried to glance back behind me and saw nothing on the roadway. But it was foggy and dark so I might not have been able to see it.

I called my wife when I got to work and asked her if she had seen anything in the road (she leaves for work right after me). She had not seen a thing.

I looked closely again at the scene of the assault on my way home and saw nothing. The attacker had made a clean getaway. Opossums are the other brown meat and taste like chicken (I would imagine). Otherwise, they can be just another large, rodent looking, Unidentified Flying Marsupial obstacle in the road. Most of the time, you only get to see them with their little feet sticking up stiffly. Yep, they are just another obstacle you have to watch out for while riding a motorcycle in the Texas suburbs.

What are the morals to this story? Be prepared at any time, any place, and under any conditions to react to changes in road conditions or obstacles in your path. Also remember, that not all obstacles hold still for you. Sometimes obstacles have a mind of their own. My UFM did.

—Torch

35. Song of the Rolling Sirens

It was a dark spring morning and a blanket of ominous clouds hovered low in the sky, making the air thick with humidity. I started the V-Star, and her 1063cc V-twin engine roared to life as I hit the garage door opener button to close the garage. It was 6 a.m., and I was hoping my neighbors did not hate me and my Cobra exhaust as I turned out of the driveway and started on my commute to work.

As I passed the local Waffle House on my way to the freeway, the odors of waffles, eggs, sausage, and bacon beckoned me to stop and eat.

I sighed at what was not to be as I approached a traffic light, downshifting twice to turn onto the access road to get on the on-ramp to the two lane freeway. Three quarters of the way up the on-ramp, my left turn signal was on as I shifted into third. I decided that the most fun part of any ride was accelerating up to speed. After all, there are no laws that limit how fast you can get up to the speed limit. In no time, I was at the end of this stretch of highway as it made a graceful right hand turn and merged with another section, this time three lanes wide.

Tending to run faster than other traffic, I applied my left turn signal and changed lanes twice, double-checking the lane next to me each time before changing.

119

In the fast lane, I pulled in right behind another motorcyclist traveling slightly faster than me, possibly on a Harley-Davidson by the sound of the engine. I sped up a little to keep up with the other motorcyclist. Traffic was usually not too bad this time of the morning as long as you did not get stuck behind a row of vehicles all traveling the same speed so that you couldn't get by in the fast lane. Some people will just not change lanes, even though slower traffic is supposed to keep right. Then, I started to hear the song.

An eighteen wheeler was in the middle lane, and I was passing on the left, tracking in the left hand side of my lane. As I drew closer, the sound of their song got louder. I glanced at all those wheels, each one almost half as tall as me. These Sirens were calling to me, luring me to look at them. I tried to look away.

Mistress, my bike, said, "Watch where we are going!"

We were approaching a left hand curve on the highway. I moved my position to the right side of my lane preparing to take the curve, doing the outside-inside-outside track thing like I don't know how tight the curve is. That placed me right next to the Leviathan's rear trailer wheels.

I glanced over, and the Sirens' song was sweeter, louder, and calling me closer as I strained to look away. "Look away, don't stare at the beast," I said to myself, probably out loud.

I was slightly behind the rig's two sets of double tires, and nearing the apex of the curve. The muscles in my legs and arms tightened up and got stiff as the Sirens' voices started screaming louder at me as I fought to avert my eyes and turn my bike away from our deadly track. All I needed to do was pull back slightly on the right handlebar, and Mistress would respond by leaning left and turning left out of that outer track, but I found myself fighting the Sirens' hypnotic song.

The Sirens' song was a screaming crescendo that pulled at Mistress and tried to make us crash against the mighty Leviathan.

My pulse quickened, and my breathing almost stopped as I tried to force her to turn left, fighting against the handlebars that felt like hard taffy. She did not respond to manhandling and awaited the gentle countersteering command.

The bike was then at the apex of the curve, and we were sliding slowly closer into the mouth of the deadly Leviathan. We were being drawn in, pulled by the voices of the alluring Sirens.

Then, Mistress' soothingly soft sultry voice cut through the panic brought about by the song of the Sirens telling me, "Look away from the beast to where you want to go."

This was said not as an order, but in a matter-of-fact, common sense way. Nodding in agreement I heard her and obeyed. Ignoring the Sirens' command, I forced my eyes to look away into the far left track of my lane. I relaxed my arms and gently pushed the left handle bar forward while pulling slightly back on the right. Mistress responded with a purr and immediately leaned left and headed into the left track, out of the deadly path of the stampeding Leviathan.

I blocked out the compelling song of the Sirens and sped by the eighteen wheeled monster, right as the corner ended.

Breathing once again, and with my pulse starting to slow, I took the exit to work. Once at work and calmed down, I had time to reflect on what had just transpired on my normal boring commute.

Call it what you want, Target Fixation or the Song of the Siren, your bike will go, maybe subconsciously, where you look. Is Target Fixation just an excuse, a myth, or an urban legend? Having battled it first hand and won, I think not.

So, glance at obstacles just long enough to recognize them for what they are; and then look back where you want to go. If you don't, you may succumb to the call of the Sirens, and smash into the very obstacle you are staring at, and trying desperately to avoid. Ride on.

—Torch

36. First Kick

You may find that certain people you meet will affect you and the path that you may be currently following. They can sneak up on you and have such a profound influence on you that they may change the rest of your life.

Growing up, I was lucky enough to know an old biker who lived directly across the road from me. He put up with me pestering him about how to fix this and fix that. Old Jack was an amazing bloke, with a grey beard, nearly white pony tail, and pale blue eyes that could cut you in half with a single glance.

Now Old Jack was a law unto himself, rough, and a man who lived life his way without any apology to anyone. He did not suffer fools, and could be mean as a bulldog chewing nettles when crossed.

My father was killed when I was just four years old and, fortunately for me, Old Jack decided to fill the role after I got into a little trouble. I guess he felt sorry for me and my mother when I kept getting brought home in a squad car time after time before I reached the age of ten.

Jack had left Ireland in '39 at the age of 19 and gone to England to fight the just war against the Nazis. He joined the British Army and became a dispatch rider, and thus started a lifelong love affair with motorcycles.

He served in several campaigns during the war, from North Africa up through Italy, and eventually the Normandy invasion. He went on to Hitler's Berlin where he remained in the army as a dispatch rider until he returned to England in '51, where he left the forces to work in a London bike shop. It was there he was thrown into the heady world of the new rock-n-roll, and the world of the ton-up boys, the Ace Cafe, and Brighton beach.

Because of his genius with the internal combustion engine, his talents were forever in demand. As a kid, I would listen to stories of the beauty of the Norton featherbed frame or the first Tritons or Tri-BSAs.

When Jack was in the mood—with the aid of a little Jameson and a bottle of stout—he would talk for hours about all the things he had seen, and that would be a whole different story.

In Jack's garage, he had his runner, an old Triumph Bonnie from 1968 (a little rough to look at, but mechanically sound), and a selection of bikes that were kept under a tarp that even I was never allowed to look under. I did try once, but he sent me away for a week, and told me not to come back until I was able to conduct myself with self-discipline and follow instructions.

For that whole week, I would watch him come and go on his trusted Triumph and seethe with anger that he had sent me away. But, finally, I got over myself and went back to listen, to learn, and—without realizing it—to be given something that I would end up carrying with me for the rest of my life: a code of ethics for life and the necessary tools to make my way in this crazy world.

Back in the spring of 1985, I was just a young lad with only a little over two years of experience riding bikes. I had owned two bikes that were bought for patience and had to be worked on before they could even be considered roadworthy. The first was a Honda 50 and the second a Kawasaki KE125.

The 50 was reliable enough but had no street cred. The traillie was respectable enough but would not go in the rain, and would overheat in the summer. It was similar to a 3TA Triumph chop I had later in life—that I tried my utmost to get along with—but I ended up shooting it with a shotgun in a drunken haze of temper one night—the less said about that, the better.

So there I was, sitting in my mother's garage working on that poor traillie, unaware that something was about to transpire that would alter my life forever.

Old Jack was 65 at this stage and getting on. Time had taken its toll, and he had stopped riding two years beforehand due to severe arthritis. He was also using a walking stick.

As I sat on the ground looking into the semi-dismantled carburetor of my Kwak, I saw Old Jack across the road waving me over, and I struggled off the garage floor and limped over with a leg that was half asleep.

I must have looked like a freaky zombie making my way to him because his face lit up with that wide old toothless grin that always meant he had some quick quip or remark ready to throw out.

"Oh look, it is Douglas Bader," he teased.

"Fuck off!" I replied, grinning like a demented fool trying to stay upright.

"I need you to do me a favour."

"Sure," I nodded. "Anything you want. What's up?"

He pointed to his shed door and asked me to open it. After pulling back the large sliding door, I looked in at the old Triumph sitting there, the spotless workshop, and the tarp-covered bikes I was never allowed to look at, but burned me with intense curiosity every time I saw them.

"I need you to get these running again," he said as he stroked his beard with his scrunched up arthritic hand, smiling at me because he knew he had just made my day, year, decade, and millennium with just one statement.

I was on my way to the promised land. I was about to see what was under the tarp. But being a teenager and trying to be cool, I simply and dumbly replied, "No sweat."

"I shall brew up then," he replied as he turned around and headed toward the house.

I felt like I had just discovered the Holy Grail. I was at my own personal Mecca.

I stood there looking at the large green, ex-military tarp, savoring the moment, trying to remember everything about all the wild fantasies of bikes that would be under it. I walked over to the mound of green, reached out and started to lift the cover off. I tried not to look until I had unveiled the entire treasure.

I stood there, silently, and just stared. Here after years of guessing, fantasizing, and concocting all sorts of dream bikes, was the answer to the puzzle.

In front of me was indeed a golden nugget, well, three to be precise. I saw a 3HW Triumph, a full blown Triton, and the jewel in the crown, a 1969 Shovelhead Harley with mini apes and fishtails, sitting there in its lovely crimson red. I had never seen three more beautiful motorcycles in my life.

I wheeled them around the garage so I would have space to walk around and take in the detail of each bike, but no matter what I did, I kept returning to the Harley. It was like a magnet. It just sucked me in and called my name. It seemed to be whispering to me to start it.

"Tea?" said Old Jack as he brought me back to reality.

"Where, when, how?" I said. I wanted to know everything all at once.

"All in good time," was all he would say.

After much chat with tea that was so black and strong it could nearly have been a soup, I talked him into letting me do the Shovelhead first.

He was freely giving advice, and telling me about the bike as I walked around it, trying to take it all in but not retaining any of it. I was in awe of the Teardrop S&S carb and air filter, the big polished primary drive with swirly engraving on it, the shape of the tank, and the curve of the seat. There was nothing I could find to fault the bike. It was just sex on two wheels. Every fiber in my young body was bursting with lust and excitement. I wasted no time and set about to get this thing of beauty going.

First, I changed all the oils, plugs, and air filter under Old Jack's watchful eye and sage advice, following each instruction as if my life depended on it. Out of the corner of my eye, I could see him watch approvingly as I spun spanner with the skill he had spent years instilling in me. After seeing to the brakes and oiling this and lubing that, the time was fast approaching to start the hunk of Milwaukee iron that was sitting on the bike lift.

I lowered the Harley to the ground and felt my heart pounding. I thought it was going to jump out of my chest and start leaping around the shed like a little alien life form. The Shovel sat there on its jiffy stand, waiting, beckoning me, wanting to be brought back to life.

I had never kick-started a Harley before, and listened carefully as old Jack imparted his wisdom. I went around to the bike and got on it. Old Jack watched with much amusement. "What was so funny?" I thought to myself. I stood there, bike between my legs, hands on the bars, and took a deep breath. Now was it two twists of the throttle and choke and kick, or was it choke, two twists and kick? Shit, why had I not listened more carefully?

Old Jack could see the indecision written all over my face and helpfully roared, "Get on with it boy!"

Right-two-throttle-choke-and-kick, I decided. I twisted the throttle all the way back twice, pulled up the choke, stood up on the kicker and jumped down on it with all my ten stones, and as much force as I could muster. I came down left foot on the floor, the right foot pushing the kicker to its final limit, but the motor did not fire. Instead, the kicker came back up hurling my knee right into my face at the top warp factor of the Starship Enterprise, breaking my nose, and splattering blood everywhere.

As the black spots receded, my vision returned, and the searing pain started to ease. All I could hear was Old Jack's wheezy laugh as he stuck a Major cigarette in his wrinkled mouth.

I felt like such a fool. I wanted the ground to swallow me up, envelop me, and leave no trace.

Having made an idiot of myself in front of my hero, just broke me. I did not know whether to cry or be pissed off that he was laughing at me. He lit his stubby cigarette and then told me that I had just learnt a valuable lesson, and to never, ever, try to start a real bike the way I just did. That was OK for those modern pieces of crap that they build for the namby-pambies you hang out with who will move out of bikes when they can afford a jammer. He did not hold some of my friends in very high esteem, and as it turned out, he was very correct. Out of 20 of us who started on bikes together, only two of us stuck with it.

So, without any fuss, I stepped to the right hand side of the bike, and did as I was told, blood cascading from my nose. I didn't care. I was mad now. This bitch was going to start or get fucking kicked into the garage floor.

I twisted the throttle, pulled up the choke, and with my left foot, leapt on the kicker. She coughed and blew two belches of blue smoke out the fishtail exhaust pipes. I let the kicker back up, gave two twists of the throttle, jumped down on the kicker, and again she coughed, blew out two plumes of bluish smoke, but refused to fire. Old Jack watched on in amusement, grinning at the fact that I was getting mad, but was still trying. I was not going to wimp out.

Once again, I gave her two blips of the throttle, jumped on the kicker, blood from my nose spraying up into my eyes, and all over the shed as I descended on the firing arc. As my right foot hit the floor of the workshop, there was a loud bang, closely followed by another, and the old Harley burst into life. The noise nearly scared the crap out of me. She was rumbling to life.

The shed filled with the beautiful sound of a running V-twin motor. It's a sound that still excites me the same way every time I start any Harley. The roar from the pipes was deafening. It shook right through me, filling me with a very strange feeling of pride, awe and power. It left me feeling like my chest was going to explode, and my head was going to be launched off my shoulders like a rocket from NASA to the moon. I have never felt that high in my life before. I stood there energized with a blood encrusted face and clothes, a bizarre looking being by all accounts.

Old Jack just looked at me with an even wider grin. He got off the stool and gestured for me to kill the motor and follow him. We went to the kitchen, and he cleaned the blood off my face. Then he explained why he had let me make a mess of myself.

"I could have told you how to do it beforehand, but you would have made that mistake somewhere down the line and done it in front of people you did not want to do it in front of," he said as he pulled on his cigarette. "Now you will never, ever start a Harley wrong again. You understand?"

When he had finished, he uttered the best words he had ever said to me: "Go out there and start her up and take her for a test ride. Don't brake too heavily as she will slide out from underneath you, OK?"

The excitement returned instantly. "Holy shit; he's going to let me ride her," I thought.

I went out to the shed like a dog in heat, or as Old Jack would say, "Faster than hot shit off a shovel."

I primed her, kicked her, and carefully took her out onto the road. I felt alive. I felt free. I rode up around the village, back past the park, past the Garda (police) station (rattling their windows with aggressive throttle control), up the new road, and back into the driveway, all in all, about five miles.

I sat in the garage telling Old Jack about my first spin, like I had just ridden in from Outer Mongolia or California to New York. I told him how the bike handled, leaving out no detail, especially the bit about the two cops running out of the station to see what was disturbing their afternoon nap. He laughed with me and told me: "Today, you have become a man. There is nothing you cannot do or accomplish. You are now the master of your own destiny."

A strange look came over his face, and his eyes were sad. I realized that he was both happy for me, and for what I had just done, but he was never going to be able to do that again. All of a sudden, I jumped up, grabbed hold of him and hugged him. "Come on, we are going out," I said. He looked at me quizzically.

I fired up the old Shovel, got on, and handed him an open face helmet. His eyes suddenly became alive. He was trembling with anticipation. He struggled with his boney, old hands to put the lid on. When I offered to help him, he just shouted back some profanity that I could not hear over the bike, and then with superhuman effort, the old man got on the bike behind me, and off we went.

After 30 miles, we were back in the driveway. I set down the side stand, hopped off, got his walking stick, and helped him off the bike.

We sat for hours in the workshop, him with his bottle of porter and his whiskey, me with my tea, listening to stories, some he had never told before because they were only for men, and some that I had listened to before since I was a boy.

I always think of Old Jack and the way he stepped in to take on the father figure role and prevent me from becoming a lesser human being.

To this day, I carry with me the code of being both a man and a biker that he taught me. Every time I start a Harley and go for a ride, he is with me. Every time I find myself in a difficult situation or have to make an important decision, I ask: "What would Old Jack do?" and in my head, I hear his answer, some 26 years later.

I often wonder what he would make of modern Harleys. Indeed, I can hear his answer sometimes as I push the starter button on my Night Train. He would probably look at me under his grey bushy eyebrows, grin widely and call me a lazy shit! I can honestly say that when Old Jack passed away a few years later, it was the first time I ever felt pain that penetrated all the way to my very being and blackened my soul a little, for the world was a darker place without him.

Old bikers have a lot they can pass on to us, and they live on with us every time you fire up a motorcycle. So, the next time an old biker sits beside you at the bar or at a table at a bike event, give them a bit of time. You never know. You might learn something.

"What happened to the Shovel?" I hear you ask. Well, my friends, that story remains to be written.

—Dyna

37. Sweet Revenge

A few years ago, I attended the first big charity run of the summer. It attracted many participants.

There was a free breakfast, midday lunch, and a grill-out later that night. It was a whole-day event that covered several hundred miles. The stops along the way had donated money to the charity in exchange for several hundred riders stopping in to patronize their businesses.

The run was in two waves. I paid my fees, got my breakfast, and sat down at a small table with two chairs. A few minutes later, a female voice asked if she could sit down and join me. She stated there were no other places to sit. I naturally told her, "Please be my guest." I looked at her and saw a very attractive Chinese girl. She was tall, about 5'-10". As we ate, we chatted about our bikes, the run, and other things.

Most big group events seem always to have a loud mouth guy you can hear above all the other noise. This event was no exception. I didn't know the guy but had heard and seen him around for several years. One of his things—besides being loud—was to get laughs by embarrassing someone.

My new breakfast friend, Sue, decided to ride alongside of me and get to be friends. This was OK with me as she was very attractive and a feast for my old eyes. At the first stop, loud mouth started on a guy he knew and his wife. He loved to get laughs as he embarrassed them. Sue did not like this, and stated that someone should teach him a lesson.

The next stop was the midday stop, halfway through the event. Sue and I made cold cut sandwiches, and took them outside to eat. Sue ate about half of her sandwich and then got up and walked over to big mouth's bike. She took something from her vest pocket and tore off the top of something. The packet was poured on the ground on both sides of the bike. Then she poured whatever it was on the gas tank. She threw the empty packet papers on the ground on both sides of the bike. She came back and finished her sandwich and drink. She disposed of our waste and sat back down next to me.

Soon old loud mouth came out to his bike and began screaming profanities. "Someone sugared my bike," he yelled. No one had put any sugar in his tank. It was just set up to look that way.

We left without loud mouth. About six weeks later, I saw loud mouth at another run, and he was unusually quiet and polite. I heard him say, "It needed rebuilding anyway."

I saw Sue off-and-on that summer, and we rode together quite often. Sue and I were only friends, because of our big age difference.

I guess if there's a moral to this story, it could be: "Just a spoonful of sugar helps the loud mouth go down."

—Edeee2

38. Where There's Smoke

We were returning home from the first ride of the long awaited spring time here in New Hampshire. A few miles from home, I spotted something alarming in the open bed of a parked truck. The truck was in a driveway with the driver's door open. Now there is nothing unusual about that, but what was strange was the small column of smoke rising from the bed of the truck.

I wondered if my wife saw the same thing, but I couldn't confirm this as she was riding behind me on her bike. Not wanting to make any sudden moves, I rode on until I came to a safe spot to pull over.

I stopped; she pulled up next to me, and I flipped open my helmet. I asked her, "Did you see the smoke rising out of that truck?" She said no, but asked if we should go back? Whether it was curiosity or the Good Samaritan in me, I thought that we should go back.

Turning around, we rode back, pulled up to the driveway, and found a safe place to park in front of the house. We honked our horns, hoping to alert the owner to our presence and the fire in the back of his truck.

Most of the time when you see smoke, it's coming from a usual source, such as a chimney or campfire, not from the back of a truck. After dismounting and taking off my helmet, I called out repeatedly, "Anyone there? Hello." There was no answer.

The truck was parked in front of an open garage, just far enough away that I still couldn't see what was burning inside the truck's bed. But that column of smoke continued its steady rise into the air.

I imagined that the owner, getting close to home, might take a final drag on a cigarette, and then toss it out the window, not realizing that the butt had reached the bed of a truck, and had now ignited some straw. Today might be the worst day of his life, with this careless cigarette destroying at least the truck, and possibly, his garage and home.

Without receiving any answer to my call, I ran up the driveway to the side of the truck. Peering in, I saw the cause of the smoke—not what I expected. There were no flames, but the column of smoke had not increased in size the whole time.

The source of the smoke was a Smudge pot. I had never even seen one before. I soon found out that it was being readied to subdue bees in the farmer's hives.

The man finally appeared at his door with a puzzled look on his face. Who were these nitwits in his yard, and what did they want? After we had explained ourselves, he thanked us for our concern, and told us he had lit the pot, put it in the bed of the truck, and then had gone to use his bathroom before walking to the field. He never thought about what the smoke might look like coming up from the truck.

We had a good laugh, and he gave us a small jar of honey for our troubles.

Therefore, when you see smoke, there's NOT always fire. You might just see a bunch of calm bees making honey.

—Jim

39. RawHyde Adventure

Last summer, I got an e-mail about an upcoming presentation at a local motorcycle dealership. It was called "Riding Beyond Where the Pavement Ends." "OK," I thought. "That sounds interesting. What harm could come from sitting through a presentation?" So that evening, my wife, Ival, and I showed up.

The enthusiastic speaker from RawHyde Adventures showed slides of desert and mountain scenery accessible by paved roads. Then he showed slides of what you could see by riding a few miles past the end of the pavement. WOW! "The idea," the speaker said, "is to get the skills to ride off-road, get a peer group to ride with, and go see what lurks beyond the edge of the asphalt!"

Ival looked over at me and—noticing that my eyeballs were bulging out of their sockets—said, "So ... I see you want to do this!"

Now I had been off-road before (yes, on purpose), mostly in Ohio where I picked up a 200cc dual sport to ride the back way to my daughter's house and to explore local roads without dread should I run out of pavement. I even took the Motorcycle Safety Foundation (MSF) "DirtBike School" course. It was mostly similar to the street course except you rode in the dirt and learned to stand while riding to counterbalance—not countersteer—to turn. But these guys were showing big touring bikes going where only mules had gone before!

With my survival instincts, common sense and sales resistance depleted, I signed up for "Introduction to Adventure" and the overnight camping trip that immediately followed. We would be going to Base Camp Alpha where I would be able to utilize these

135

newly learned skills in the "real world." This event was scheduled for January. Fortunately for me, it would be in sunny California. I'd probably only need to wear my mesh jacket—wrong!

The people at RawHyde were very helpful and suggested I could send my riding gear out ahead by FedEx. I checked the expected January weather online, and it looked like temperatures mostly in the 40-60 degree range with an overnight in the low 30s on Monday (the night in the desert at Base Camp Alpha). I thought better about the mesh gear and took a bunch of jacket liners, my winter textile jacket, off-road boots, off-road helmet and goggles, turtle furs, and "Joan of Arc" balaclava.

E-mails began flying among the participants and—with the help of the RawHyde staff—we arranged to share a van ride to the camp. I arrived at LAX three hours later than local time since my body was still on EST. A few texts and cell calls later, we were all in the van and on the way. Some like me were taking an introductory course, but others were taking an advanced course and going on a longer expedition. Everyone was excited and friendly, and we persuaded the driver to stop to get a bite to eat to hold us till dinner. We stopped at a little sandwich store and got (what was purported to be) the best thing they sold. It was a pastrami sub with mustard and salad (make that cucumbers and salsa). Hunger may be the best sauce, as I found it delicious!

A short ride later, we arrived at the foot of the most intimidating driveway—and I am very generous to call it a driveway—made of potholed, broken, non-connected, off-cambered strips of asphalt interspersed with dirt, mud, gravel and—who knows how deep— potholes. It snaked up the hill with signs pointing out the "cliff" at the edge of one switchback.

We arrived at the headquarters, signed in at the "office"—a double-wide trailer with a couple of bathrooms and bedrooms for two lucky employees.

I got a prime assignment in the "bunkhouse." Others got assigned to trailers and tents, or some mutant monstrous hybrid of both!

The bunkhouse had a concrete slab floor, real walls, and windows—but a tent for a roof.

Showers were outdoors with a great view of the mountains—but not each other.

Pretty soon it was happy hour and time to introduce ourselves to the group and meet the instructors and staff. Dinner followed, prepared by a great chef. They easily accommodated my kosher style and low carb diet as well as someone's vegetarian preferences. Then off to music around the campfire and turn-in at 1 a.m. EST (10 p.m. PST).

Next morning after breakfast, we got assigned our rental bikes— mine was a BMW GS1200 Adventure—and listened to the lecture/demonstration on riding. In no time, they had us mount up and head down the so-called driveway, standing on the pegs. With no real previous experience on an unfamiliar off-road bike that seemed SO HUGE, it was some miracle that we all made it down, paddled through a U-turn on the street, and then made a return trip up the driveway. Oh, and then we all went down and up again, moving around on the bike swinging a leg over one side or the other while standing on one foot peg.

The rest of the training exercises are all blurred in my mind. We went down the driveway again and then down to the dirt approach road to do rear wheel skidding. We walked the bike up the hill in first gear. We almost locked up the front wheel with the brake. We made a panic stop on dirt. We performed more uncountable drills in the dirt. (One of us fell over and rolled around in obvious pain. Eventually, the word got back that he was not seriously hurt having only "crushed his rocks" and that continued as a good-natured ribbing the rest of the weekend.)

All of us fell over more times than I can count. If you touched the front brake on a slippery surface, the wheel locked and flipped you to the ground—instantly. I think I had the dishonor of being the first to fall, but it was of no lasting shame. At some point, there was lunch and a drill on the serpentine dirt path cone weave which I thought would make a pretty good video game with all the flopping over and picking up going on.

We learned to drag, twist, and slide the bike into a better position to allow us to pick it up using the slope of the hill to our advantage. (Don't try to slide your bike on pavement.) We learned the usual butt-in-the-seat method and also the horse-it-up-by-the-handlebar method.

Dinner came and was superb once again. The chef did something to Brussels Sprouts that made them one of the best foods I had ever eaten!

We each shared the high and low points of the day. Then, we headed off to bed, aching and limping.

The next day, we reviewed the previous day's triumphs and tragedies, and then we went to the wooded hill to do the off-camber cone weave course, both up and down hill. We had more dropping-of-the-bike along the way, but it seemed that, at low speeds in the dirt, no one got hurt. We went up to the sand whoops at the top of the hill to practice stopping on top of each earthen hummock, and then under control, on to the next one. I watched the rider in front of me fall over at zero mph while waiting his turn. How could that happen?

I then repeated the same stunt but enhanced it by smacking my intake manifold into the instructor's rear wheel, dislodging the intake. The bike refused to run at anything but wide open throttle, so we switched bikes, and as it was time for lunch, he coasted my wounded bike down a steep hillside while I rode on down to the paddock. It turned out that my throttle cable under the tank got caught on something in the fall, and that was why the bike wouldn't idle properly.

Next, part way down the driveway, we made a sharp left through the bushes and downhill into the meadow. Then, we had everyone's favorite exercise: figure-8 U-turns in a box and the—always popular—figure-8 off-camber drill!

I killed a bunch of cones but no trees or instructors. Did I mention I dropped the bike a few more times? But the real treat was the big outside loop around the meadow on the dirt. That's what I call fun!

Later we learned to go up and down the hill under control and do a trail-stop (to see which way the road goes—left, right, or straight). Then we would do a downhill where front brake is allowed due to a shift in weight putting more pressure on the front wheel so it won't lock up. Learning to start on a hill was wild. You popped the clutch in first to act as an emergency brake, and then used the rear brake to hold you while you revved the engine and played with the clutch to get going without wheel spin.

My biggest problem was I couldn't seem to get the rear brake to work. My right foot turns out (flue foot) so I need to concentrate to make it toe-in to find the brake pedal. I thought I was pushing on the brake, but the bike wouldn't hold on the hill and wouldn't slow enough to stop when I was approaching a stopped rider. Rather than crash into someone, I tried to use the very slightest amount of front brake pressure, but the bike flopped over every time! It wasn't good for my confidence—my ego died a long time ago!

After the exercises, I rode back up the hill part way and then did a 179 degree right turn between the barbed wire and the edge of the road, onto a path between boulders, grazing cows and horses. Someone dropped a bike ahead. The two riders ahead of me dismounted to go help, and as I tried to dismount on the off-camber terrain, I dropped my bike ... again.

Then we went back downhill and up the driveway but made a left this time onto the cell tower road. It was severely rutted and muddy and of course, I managed to drop it in the mud twice on the way up, the last time within sight of the cell tower, but I couldn't get it started on the muddy hill. The instructor rode it up the last 20 feet, but I was feeling very tired and decided to call it a day at about 4:30 p.m., skipping the last trail ride and the sand pit.

In 20/20 hindsight, I should have continued on (more speculation later on), but I figured that I had the expedition to Base Camp Alpha ahead of me, and so far I had not gotten hurt, so I called in wisdom as the better part of valor. However, this meant I had to go down the muddy, rutted cell tower road following the instructor and one other rider who needed to head back early, coasting down engine-off most of the way, trying to follow his line—all this with my insecure rear braking ability.

Happy hour beer, hors d'oeuvres, and dinner came along with a graduation certificate presentation. We celebrated with the house brand RawHyde wines. Tomorrow, our adventure would get serious.

Next morning, we packed our sleeping bags, blankets, towels, and any additional gear or personal items we had, onto the trucks heading for Base Camp Alpha. I took every liner and shirt I had since the forecast was for 30 degrees overnight.

We headed out on the interstate, losing one rider to electrical gremlins (he fixed it and joined us later), then onto local roads, refueling in Mojave, California, witnessing a parking lot flat tire repair, then headed off to California City for a lunch stop. It was right at the edge of the desert, and the wind did blow! A fine lunch was provided by the staff at the chuck wagon truck.

Then we had an outdoor pit stop (watch out which way the wind blows!) and our first ride onto the sand! Or maybe it was the second ride. My memory is a little hazy because we may have already been in the western edge of the Mojave desert following the Aqueduct trail. But I do remember the wind by the windmill farms. (Why do you suppose they have the windmills located where the wind never seems to stop blowing?)

There were mountains visible in the distance, and you could see the clouds pouring over them like shaving cream overflowing. Yes, it was cold when the wind blew, but you got warm since you worked so much harder standing and riding off-road than you did on the road.

At some point, we went back on the pavement, then off again for a little while and back to asphalt along some wonderful curving roads with great views of the green and purple mountain majesties. I needed to remind myself to pay attention to the road as I was easily distracted by the scenery. We took a break in a ghost town complete with a mill used to separate the gold ore.

Meanwhile, I had a zipper failure on the leg of my riding pants, so the material was billowing in the wind, open from hip to ankle. A kindly local offered up a roll of duct tape so I could seal it at the knee. One of the other riders helped apply the tape, but I think he misunderstood its purpose since he was wrapping it tight enough to be a tourniquet! I loosened it some, and it served its purpose. I could wiggle my leg out of the pants and boot, and then back into them when the time came and no more flapping!

We refueled once more and finally arrived at Base Camp Alpha. It seems that the Chinese laborers—who, you remember, built the railroads, and cooked and supplied all the gold rush prospectors—had built "sleeping circles." These circles were areas where the ground was leveled, and small stones were piled up about 8-12 inches high to block the wind. We pitched the supplied tents and foam pads in circles of this kind. We raced to get the tents together before we lost the daylight. I had never seen that particular tent before (remember camping rule #1: always try to put up your tent at home, so you learn its quirks in a light comfortable environment, not in the rain or the dark!). I did great except for getting the tent fly on backwards. I straightened it out just as dusk arrived, and then we had a campfire and a real *Blazing Saddles* dinner.

The full moon peeked slowly over the mountains and rose in the sky as night fell. The stars were so numerous and intense as diamonds scattered on black velvet! Words failed to capture the beauty of it. Three of us took turns playing our guitars, and it was interesting because our music overlapped in time. Mine was Beatles, early Dylan, and folk music. The other two favored artists from the next two decades, had loved the same (or similar) artists I did, and we all liked the same kind of folk, folk/rock, and acoustic rock genre. Even so, we did all agree that we were not ready to quit our day jobs just yet, but we enjoyed our guitar "gig" around the campfire.

We had an early breakfast and those of us who were returning to RawHyde HQ, packed up their tents, while those on extended expeditions would spend one more night at Alpha. My group was heading for the desert to see the Trona Pinnacles.

They were made 10,000 to 100,000 years ago by underwater combinations of ground water and alkaline lake water that grew tufa formations. After the water had receded, the Trona Pinnacles remained. The scene was truly otherworldly, and this fact was not lost on movie makers (remember LA is not far away). Some *Star Trek* episodes and *Planet of the Apes* scenes were filmed here. I turned around to leave and did one more obligatory drop-of-the-bike in the deep sand.

On we went across the plain to a very steep rocky hill. I was told just to pick a good line without too many rocks, probably start out on the left and finish the hill on the right. It was very, very spooky looking, but I grit my teeth, tried to relax, feathered the clutch and throttle and stayed off the brakes. Momentum was my savior. The bike slowed as it rolled over a large rock in my path, but I learned to let the big girl (GSA1200) dance beneath my feet by playing with the throttle, and also keeping the clutch in the friction zone.

There was a burning smell, rubber or clutch (I don't know which), but I was determined and focused and made it up the hill. My sunglasses inside my special goggles (made to fit over glasses) had completely steamed up so I couldn't see well. The desert around me was fragrant with a mix of smoking bike parts and my personal "flop sweat." I removed the offending sunglasses and stripped a layer off since I was now feeling very warm. I took my camelback-equipped small backpack with me and figured that it was time to rehydrate.

Next up was the sand whoops, a series of undulating hills with deeper sand at the bottom of each hill. I have seen motocross guys double and triple jump these, but our technique was just to ride them out one at a time, staying loose and keeping balanced. It was the most fun I had so far, and my confidence soared. We reached a paved road and headed for lunch near Jawbone Canyon. At first the breeze at speed was a delight, but as the miles wore on, I wished I had my layer back and my warmer gloves. Again at our lunch stop, the kitchen staff from RawHyde provided another tasty treat.

We had a choice of routes home for the afternoon. We could go across Jawbone Canyon on its roads up and down the hills, and then spend an hour on the freeway—with the trucks. Or, we could go on some roads down to Ruby Canyon with its switchbacks and water crossings, and then on some nice local roads back to RawHyde. The group voted to avoid the freeway.

We mounted up and refueled back in Mojave, and then got lost trying to get to Ruby Canyon. The road was long, straight, and flat. The wind was blowing continually. I was having some issues with muscle cramps in my leg. I tried to stretch and change positions to no avail, so I slowed down and pulled over at a stop sign. My fellow riders and instructors immediately inquired about my condition, but I was hoping maybe it was because I got a little dehydrated, or I needed more carbohydrates for energy. I was working harder than I usually do and in a much dryer climate than I was used to. I swigged probably half the contents of my camelback and scarfed down a bag of cheese crackers from my jacket. That seemed to do the trick. I would need to remember to drink more and to get a mid-afternoon snack in the future. I bet the previous day's tiredness in the late afternoon had a similar origin.

We rode some beautiful, curvy paved roads and pulled over at the entrance to Ruby Canyon. We headed down a steep dirt road, filled with ruts and rocks, with a cliff on one side. At the bottom was a steep downhill-to-uphill switchback, and I was not feeling good about it.

I went wide into the deeper dirt on the right side. One of the instructors came by and said, "You don't look like you are having any fun. Loosen up and counterbalance the bike as you were taught." He offered to have me follow him in a little monkey-see monkey-do drill and then, I did much better. I was extremely grateful for his help.

Next we headed down, and the trail was muddier and rutted. I got stuck in a rut and flipped to the ground once again, muddied but unbowed. Ahead another rider was pannier-deep in a mud puddle on his side. Others came to his aid. He was not hurt, but the bike had battle-scarred auxiliary lights. I decided to avoid that track and began to get adept at switching tracks. We came to our first water crossing, but it was not deep enough to satisfy our instructors. They went on ahead to scout out the next crossing down the route. That was much more to their liking. We all negotiated the first crossing and pretty soon lined up for the next one where there was a camera to document our semi-aquatic foray. We got up enough momentum to get across, no turning, no brakes, eyes on the prize, across the water—no problem. A short ride up the road and we were back to the pavement on another curvy road.

On cue, the sun began to set between the mountain peaks, a perfect counterpoint to the desert moonrise the night before. Now the sky turned a deep cerulean blue, and the clouds turned contrasting pink. Another curve in the road and I snapped my consciousness away from scenic beauty and back to riding. How strange it seemed now to weight the inside of the turns and countersteer! Not to worry, as darkness fell, I came upon the RawHyde driveway, now occupied by an ambling horse.

We went around a switchback where a cow was grazing, blocking half the width of the road. I managed to get back to the paddock and pat my bike farewell. It may have been happy to see me go— or maybe not. (I finally figured out that if I sat back a little, more weight came to the rear brake and made stopping more effective. Or maybe muscle memory finally found the friggin' pedal!) I wondered how the next camper/adventurer would do on this bike.

Some of my riding colleagues (who lived locally) packed up and headed for home. The rest of us enjoyed one last wonderful dinner—celebrated with RawHyde wine—with the most fabulous dessert of broiled Banana S'mores Swans.

The atmosphere was supportive in that the instructors knew we were trying our best even if we were not 100 percent successful at everything. This very special group of people got together to try something beyond their previous experience. Was it outside the box? There was no box! Was it outside the familiar? Oh yeah! Was it challenging? Was it fun? Was it rewarding? Yes, Yes, Yes!

I'm back at home now, but I'm still there in my mind (whenever my mind has a few moments to wander). I know that I have grown in my motorcycle skills. Dirt is more my friend now than ever before. However, I do need to find some local riders to join me in more off-road riding.

Uh-oh! I think I got bit by the off-road bug, and there is no known cure.

145

—Joel Storm

40. Safe Riding is No Accident

The first time I rode a motorcycle was when I was 12 years old. A younger friend of mine, Glen, who was the closest neighbor to us in the Sandia Mountains of New Mexico where I grew up, had parents who rode motorcycles. They bought Honda 150 dirt bikes for him and his sister, Dina. She never rode her bike. Somehow Glen conned me into hopping on his sister's bike, telling me that first gear was one down, and the rest of the gears were up. He also told me that the left hand controlled the clutch and the right hand controlled the front brake.

We rode down the dirt road away from his house to the main road for maybe two miles before turning around and going back. I do not believe I even shifted out of first the whole time.

Mr. Hollingsworth, Glen's dad, was waiting for us in the driveway when we got back. He was an old WW2 veteran who had the pug-nosed dogface look of an army guy like you would expect to see in a movie like *Patton*.

His body was still strong and fit from years of working, hunting, riding, and taking care of business, and his eyes seemed to see through us, as if he were looking into the past and future at the same time. His silence spoke louder than any words, and when he spoke, you listened half out of fear and half out of curiosity for what he was trying to tell you.

So, when he called us over to him, he asked us where our helmets were, and told us that motorcycles are like snakes: If you fear them they bite you, but if you don't fear them, they bite you too. He had us park the bikes, and I didn't ride a motorcycle again for more than 20 years.

His words echoed in my memory all the way to this day, however, and were good advice for any rider: "Do not fear or take for granted what you are riding, just respect it."

I didn't start riding seriously until 2003 when gas prices were hovering around $5 per gallon. I had been accepted to graduate school for biochemistry at Arizona State University in Tempe, while my wife, Erin, was accepted to graduate school for hydrology at the University of Arizona in Tucson. We decided to move to Casa Grande, which is a cow town approximately halfway between the two cities, with Erin getting a slightly longer drive than my 120 mile round trip.

I had been driving a 1978 Trans Am to and from Tempe for the first month of graduate school, but I was spending nearly $120 a week in gas transiting back and forth each day. Erin had a similar drive, so you can imagine how much we were spending on gasoline. Something had to give!

I read that motorcycles could get 50 or more miles to the gallon, and I started imagining what it would be like riding an old Harley to school. The long drive back and forth to Phoenix, each day, was boring in the car, but a motorcycle might make things interesting, as well as cheaper.

I started looking in the Arizona classifieds for a motorcycle. I wanted a classic Harley, but that was not cheap. All the ones in the paper were around $5,000 at the cheapest, and I was looking to spend around $3,000 for a starter bike.

When I found a bike I was interested in, I would call and find out that it had already been sold, just days before. I finally found a guy selling his Harley Sportster for $4,000, and he still had it in his possession. He lived in Phoenix, so one day after school I stopped by his house to look at it.

The guy's name was Kim, and he looked like the stereotypical Harley biker that would kill you if you made fun of his name. He had long gray hair and wore a beard. He also wore a bleached denim jacket and pants, and a red bandana on his head.

He said he needed the money for his sick wife, and he showed me the bike in his garage. It was a 1989 Sportster 883cc with ape hangers and a bobbed tank sporting a custom paint job of a naked black woman with big round breasts looking like they had been painted on by a nine-year-old.

He said that the bike had been modified by Sonny Barger, which meant nothing to me at the time. I didn't have $4,000 so I asked him if he would consider a trade. I had an old Remington 870 twelve gauge that I used to duck hunt with when I lived in Minnesota, and a black powder .50 cal Flintlock for hunting deer. He said he would settle for the $3,000 and those two guns. I'm sure he thought he got a better deal—which maybe he did.

But in reality, the Harley was a great starter bike. It was plain enough that it didn't matter what I did to it while I was learning to ride, but special enough that I didn't mind riding it.

The next day, we transferred the title into my name, and he loaded the bike into the back of his truck to tow it to Casa Grande. He followed behind me the entire way and dropped it off at my apartment. I put a cover over it and was the proud new owner of a leaky old Harley Sportster.

I signed up for a TEAM Arizona Motorcyclist Training class hosted on the following weekend. The class had one day of lecture and testing, one day of riding a motorcycle provided for us, and then we would be given a pass/fail for licensing.

The other unappealing option was to be tested by the DMV, which supposedly had a strict examination that had a low passing rate. I decided to pay my $100 for the TEAM examination—money well spent.

The week prior to the training class, I tested my bike out on the back roads of Casa Grande. I cannot express how valuable this experience was. There was little to no traffic on those back roads. A beginning biker needs this experience where it's just him, the bike, the road, and few other distractions.

Let me tell you, the first time you put a motorcycle in gear and pull out onto a road, you become a bad ass. You are taking your life into your own hands, and you are then the most exposed and vulnerable you will ever be. If you have any fear whatsoever of death, you had better come to grips with it before you go out riding. If you hit a dog, or if someone in a car doesn't see you and hits you while you are doing 40 mph, you might very well be at the end of the rainbow.

These things go through your mind the first time you push the starter button and feel the engine rumbling beneath you. Believe me, I felt all that while I was out testing the Harley for the first few rides.

I like to tell people that I strapped on a big set of balls before going out, and figuratively I did. I've met people since who could not overcome the fear of being snuffed out in one big fiery crash, so they only drive cars and view riding with a mix of fear and admiration.

My first time riding, I knew the Reaper was on my back seat, but I said, "Screw it. Let's go!" That's what it takes to get started riding at midlife, and if you don't have that spirit, do yourself a favor and stay in the cage.

My first time out, I was becoming accustomed to gear shifting and turning. At one point, I took one of the turns too wide and ended up in a ditch, scratching one of the boobs off the naked black girl on my tank. I think this was an improvement to the paint job, but don't tell that to Kim.

Some cowboys in a pickup truck saw me ride into the ditch and were laughing—I was quite embarrassed. But, even so, I picked up the bike and rode it around the block, getting used to its handling. I felt like a rock star, doing all of maybe 20 mph.

I felt confident enough to be able to take my riding test that weekend after riding the Harley those few times. That Saturday, I went to the lecture part of the TEAM test. Our lecturer was a big biker lady, who drove up on a Harley Fat Boy. She showed us a video, and then gave us a written exam that I passed with a perfect score.

The lecturer taught us many useful How-Tos: how to stay out of truck blind spots; how not to get into a pissing contest with a car— it always wins; and how to maintain at least a 2-second distance from cars in front of you. With the classroom training under my belt, I was ready for the driving portion of the exam on Sunday.

I remember that day in detail, because it was so much fun, at least for me. Some people decided it was not for them after only a few minutes of riding. Others were frightened every step of the training. Still others were experienced riders. And then there was me, who had just learned how to shift and ride on my Harley in Casa Grande earlier that week.

The TEAM trainers gave us a brief outdoor lecture. They told us to pay attention to everything they said, and to follow what they were teaching, to the letter. When they said stop, we were to stop. When they said go, we were to go! They said they understood that, for many of the people there, it was their first time on a motorcycle, and that was OK.

They started out showing us how to shift gears, and how to drive straight for a short distance. I did that quite easily, but for a few people, it was an ordeal. One guy, instead of putting the motorcycle into first gear, clicked it straight into fourth and stalled the bike repeatedly. He made mistakes all day, to the point where the lecturers were looking at each other, trying to decide if they should pass him. But they didn't have the heart *not to* pass him. Their thinking was: "If you have balls enough to mount up, then you can work through the rest."

They taught us how to run over objects like boards, how to brake quickly, and how to pull to the left or right in case someone slams on their brakes in front of you. I can remember the lecturer yelling to this lady to "plant your feet when you stop!" but she didn't listen, and toppled over when she stopped, knocking down several other riders, as if they were dominoes. She got up and left the training grounds, saying "This isn't for me!" even though she said earlier that she had just spent $50,000 buying a new Harley earlier that week. I remember three or four people quitting during the test, but the majority stayed.

We drove zigzag around cones, and this is when I knew I felt comfortable riding, because it went smoothly and flawlessly. I passed the riding part of the exam, as did almost everyone, even the guy who couldn't put his bike in gear at the beginning of the class, and was sweating like a waterfall under his helmet for most of the exam.

Every rider who stayed, stuck it out, and struggled to get a feel for the bike that day, was a hero to me. I thought that this break-in period was a great proving ground that gave us an excellent start.

I would like to thank the TEAM trainers for their patience that day, and for getting us all broken through the ice, into the world of motorcycling.

At the end of the day, the lecturers gave us some general suggestions, warnings, and advice. At one point, one of the lecturers said, "The car driver who is going to hit you probably won't be a high school student learning how to drive, or an old senile person in a delirium. It will be a 30ish-year-old lady listening to her stereo and talking on her cell phone, paying no attention, whatsoever, to the road." It was said as prophecy—for me, it was.

One day, my Trans Am finally had enough of the long drive to Tempe and threw a rod. All I had for transportation was my Harley. Out of necessity, I took the next big step in my bike riding experience by riding the long distance to ASU every day on my motorcycle.

There was no way in hell I was going to ride on the highway when I first started distance riding. Instead, I decided to take a back country two-lane road that led all the way into Tempe.

I took a beautiful early morning ride every day for several months. I started out when it was dark, and there were a million stars in the sky. I smelled the cactus and felt the fresh fall air cooling my skin all the way into town. I would watch the sunrise as I rode to school and the sunset as I rode home.

This was an important break-in period, where I learned how to ride at speeds around 50 mph (sometimes more!). I learned how to maneuver at speed, how to pay attention to what was in front of me, how to pass cars and be passed, how to ride in rain and wind, and how to ride in city traffic—that got progressively thicker as I got closer to school.

As the winter approached, I put on several layers of clothes under my jacket and bought some lined gloves. I rode my motorcycle through the whole cold season, riding like a scared rabbit all winter, never forgetting to fear and respect the snake lest it bites me.

At one point in the road was a turn off onto the main highway, I-10, which led into Phoenix. I passed by it every day during my back road trek, and each time I asked myself why I didn't have the courage just to turn onto the on-ramp and take I-10 into Tempe. I'd pass it by each time, afraid of what wrecking on the highway would mean. Finally, one day I strapped on an even bigger set of balls, turned onto the on-ramp, and gunned it past the point of no return.

It was exhilarating being on the highway, with the wind on my chest, pushing me back and forcing me to grip the apes harder.

For the first time going into town, I stayed in the slow lane and followed a trucker all the way to Phoenix, afraid to pass him.

It wasn't until one of the later rides that I decided to pass a semi-truck. Its wake, at first, pushed me out and then sucked me in. When I was in front of the semi, all the turbulence was gone.

Every day I was getting braver, more daring, and more stupid.

Once I got used to highway riding, I started feeling like I was a real biker. By summer, I was riding on the highway with no helmet and no leather jacket. I had only a biker hat, a pair of sunglasses, blue jeans, and my boots between me and all that asphalt.

I had since customized my bike with a new set of tie-dye tins, some custom skull mirrors, and lots of chrome.

I started doing cocky things, like riding in the HOV lane with no hands on the handlebars, popping wheelies at lights in town, and riding up to 100 mph and faster sometimes on the long ride home.

I decided to convert the 883cc engine to a 1200cc engine to get more power—a mistake. The bike shop I took it to, put the push rods in backwards and blew one of the lifters apart and into the engine casing. The bike started to "not run right" after that, and I needed a new motorcycle, since I had missed a week of school due to a breakdown and drew some negative attention upon myself for that. I went to the local bike shop in Casa Grande, where I had been buying my sunglasses, brake pads, etc. and started looking for a new bike.

I was considering a highway cruiser when I saw a 2001 Yamaha V-Max for sale. It looked unique, but the salesman told me it was not a beginner's bike. I asked my wife if we could afford it, and ended up walking away with the keys to it.

The V-Max was an incredibly fast road shark. I was glad that I had first been weaned on the Sportster, since the V-Max would buck-off an inexperienced rider like an unbroken stallion would buck-off a cowboy.

She was all black, sleek, and could easily do 140 mph on the highway, without so much as a shake or shimmy. I rode for a while without a helmet, but after a huge bug slammed into my forehead on the highway and made me see stars one day, I decided to start wearing a full face helmet.

My wife became pregnant with our daughter, and the round-trip to Casa Grande took its toll on both my wife and me. We both burned out on graduate school almost at the same time, and decided to quit school and go to work. I found a job in Phoenix and had my first accident on the way home one night.

It had been raining, and I came up to a choke point on the highway where everyone was forced to slow down. The motorist behind me was driving way too fast in his SUV, and slammed on his brakes, spinning his vehicle around in front of me. I braked hard with both front and rear brakes to avoid hitting him, and my bike toppled to the left.

The accident gouged my left hand through the leather glove and gave me a spiral fracture on my thumb. Luckily, it only broke the windshield and a mirror on my motorcycle, but the whole experience was sobering enough that I stopped being cavalier, and started following the safety tips I had learned through my TEAM training.

From then on I've kept both hands on the handlebars, and I've always worn my helmet.

I decided that riding in the Phoenix traffic was going to kill me and that I needed to find a job in Tucson so my wife and I wouldn't have such a long commute. I had my second accident soon after finding a job in Tucson, when a driver drove from the far right lane all the way to the left turn lane, cutting in front of me, and forcing me to lay my bike down.

My bike slid for maybe 100 yards before it finally came to rest. I hadn't been wearing my leather gloves, since it was my first day at my new job, and I was just going for a short ride to get new work shoes. My hands contacted the asphalt at some point, and I skinned my palms, but beyond that, I was unhurt.

A fellow biker ran to my aid after the accident, pulling my bike off the road, and helping me to the side. The driver who caused the accident did not stay at the scene. He was long gone. A fire and rescue vehicle came to the scene, patched me up, and I rode the bike home. My bike appeared to be undamaged after this dramatic slide. Even so, the insurance company totaled the bike after the adjuster evaluated the damage and found a broken front fork brace.

She had been a good bike, and I rode her for over 40,000 miles before that accident. It made me very sad the day the insurance company took her away from me.

My wife and I started looking for a car for me, and I hated them all. She asked me if I wanted to go to a bike shop instead—half as a joke—and I realized that, despite the accident, I didn't want to give up riding. We went to a local bike shop, and I bought another

V-Max, this time a 2006, with red flames, shift light, and all the geegaws you could stick onto a V-Max. I barely started to get comfortable on this bike when I had my third accident.

This time, I was at a red light in the far right lane of a Tucson city street with a truck to my left. The light turned green, and I pulled out into the intersection, when the truck to my left slammed on its brakes. I continued forward, and had just enough time to look to my left, and see a white car barrel through the intersection, and T-bone me at high speed.

The driver—a 30-year-old-lady on her cell phone, listening to her techno music, and not paying attention—had run a red light and hit me so hard that the impact scooped both me and my motorcycle onto the hood of her car. She had carried me for a short distance before she slammed on her brakes, and I slid off her hood as a pancake would off a spatula. I had been wearing my helmet which was a good thing, since my head slammed into the pavement, and the helmet took the blow. My back was twisted a bit and my leg was pinned by a bumper. Beyond that, I was unhurt. To this day, I feel that God reached down and saved me, possibly for my daughter's sake.

Had I been in my wife's car, I doubt I would have fared as well. Riding a motorcycle was a very good thing that evening. I was taken to the hospital, and released after a few hours. I was sore for the next few days, and to this day, I cannot help but think that things could have been much worse.

I've been riding for seven years now, almost every day since I got my license. Despite the accidents I've had, I still love riding. I just want riders to know that no matter how careful you are, you just never know what's going to happen. I've known this since the beginning, but the accidents have hammered it home for me, over and over.

Some advice:

Don't be silly. Wear a helmet, gloves, and something to protect your skin from the asphalt.

Keep your distance from cars, look straight ahead, and always have the mindset that the person you are looking at just might do something crazy—but that you will be ready for it. I look at every car and say, "What is the worst thing this person can do right now?" It won't happen in 9999 cases out of 10000. But when that one in 10000 case occurs, I know what I'm going to do beforehand. I believe that is why I'm still around after seven years of riding a motorcycle in traffic.

Never be in a hurry, always just chill out and enjoy the ride.

Don't be either afraid or unafraid, just respect your motorcycle.

Keep the rubber on the road, my brothers.

—Sean Blankert

41. Don't Box Me In

I was on my Honda 750 ACE heading east down I-80 to Des Moines, Iowa. I caught up with a line of four 18-wheelers that were all under the speed limit by about 5 mph.

Just as I started to pull out and pass, I double checked my mirror, and saw there was a car coming. Now I could have accelerated, and been in front of it safely enough, but I played it conservatively because a 750 is not an interstate machine.

I backed off a bit, let the car go by, and then started to move over to pass. When I backed off, the last two semis pulled out to pass the two in front of them. Not arguing with a vehicle that outweighed me by 80,000 pounds, I watched them go.

I checked my mirrors a couple of times, and didn't find anyone coming hard from behind, so I went ahead and followed them around.

MISTAKE!

They took their own sweet time getting around. (It takes a long time if you are only going five mph faster than the vehicle you are passing.) By the time the fourth truck in line got even with the first truck in line, I had a big Dodge Ram that was so close behind me, I couldn't even see his license plate.

If I had been riding two-up, my passenger could have easily turned around and slapped the hood of the Ram.

I had the wind buffeting me from the front and side from semis, and a Ram ready to ram me from behind. It was, without a doubt, one of the few times riding that I was truly scared.

I got out of it OK but learned a valuable lesson: never get yourself boxed-in.

—Milo

42. The Coke Can

Back in the late '70s I was flying for a missionary aviation group in Venezuela. My only transportation was a Honda 90—I don't remember the exact model. I rode that thing for the eight years I was there, and ten years later I heard that someone was still riding it.

In Latin America, trash is everywhere. I've often thought that the poverty problem could be solved by having the government pay for trash, with the added benefit that it would clean up the place.

One day, I was riding my Honda on a residential street, maybe 25 miles per hour, when I noticed a Coke can directly in front of me. This one was still perfect, hadn't been flattened yet. On a whim, I decided to see if I could hit it.

It happened to be perpendicular to my front wheel, so I hit it perfectly. I was feeling smug about my precision riding for about two tenths of a second, when my front wheel locked up, and I went down like a sack of potatoes.

What happened?

I picked myself up and looked at my front wheel. When the wheel rolled over the can, the ends were pulled in, and the can clamped itself to the tire, then came up and jammed itself between the forks, locking the front wheel!

A nice lady and her teenage daughter heard the crash, and came out to see if I was OK. They invited me into their house to clean up my road rash and offered me a cool drink—Coke, of course.

I never intentionally ran over a can again.

—Tumbleweed

159

43. Trip to Llano

Jill and I had talked about going camping by motorcycle for months. It was something we wanted to do together, to see places up close. Little by little we acquired all the essentials but weren't able to set a date. There was always something that prevented us from proceeding with the plan. Finally, we agreed that our destination would be Llano, Texas, and we would leave on the day after Thanksgiving, weather permitting.

A friend and colleague invited us to stay on his five-acre property in the hill country—a perfect opportunity and a safe test bed for this endeavor. I looked forward to this first trip into the wild. If everything went according to our made up scenario, it would set a precedent for future travels. This initial trial of weathering the elements of nature would make or break or even burst our bubble of camping out.

9 a.m. was "kick stand" time (in biker jargon) to get on the road. At 10 a.m., I still hadn't loaded the two bikes. Luckily we packed everything up in bags the night before. Although I "Kentucky-windaged" it, I did a pretty good job in balancing the luggage. It looked like a professional had a hand in it. Even Jill gave me a couple of taps on the shoulder for a job well done. Secretly, I thanked God for bungee cords, all 13 of them!

Zeb was constantly twinkle-toeing around the bikes, eager to jump on. Zeb is a strange dog. When I wanted him to ride with me more than a year before and taught him how to sit on the motorcycle, I never imagined he'd love it! Now every time when I have to leave without him, he always gives me a dejected look. That little critter knows how to lay on the guilt trip. It was a little windy and chilly that morning, so I put his jacket and goggles on him. The man was ready to roll. A quick short whistle and he jumped into his seat.

We tweaked a few things here and there and strapped our small backpacks to both fuel tanks. Now we were ready. About time!

The Jillster was looking forward to her first big ride. Little did I know she would develop into a speed demon! Zeb, a veteran, was all mounted up and ready to go.

We took the Bush Turnpike to I-20. Traffic wasn't bad, but the wind took us by surprise. Plus it was colder than I had anticipated, and severe wind gusts rocked us sideways—constantly. Not a good omen for things to come. The weather forecast promised warmer temperatures later in the day.

After about 35 miles, my goggles came detached from my helmet. We were doing 70 mph, and there was no way I was able to adjust it without looking for trouble—too risky. I signaled Jill to take the next exit. The military efficiency of the trip was already out the door, and it wasn't even 11:30 a.m. We pulled into a gas station parking lot where I fixed the problem.

I promised myself that I would keep a log of the trip. My wife told me to call it the "Captain's log." I liked that. Although she took the lead of the whole expedition as far as directions (I couldn't find my way out of a parking lot, even if I had a GPS), she made me feel in charge. LOL. Good old Jill. How was it again? "A man is only as strong as the woman behind him."

After Zeb had taken a quick pee behind the bushes, we were back on the road. Except for the loss of time and another dent in our schedule, it felt good being out of the wind for several minutes. We got energized by it and were able to find our bearings and brace ourselves for things ahead.

We decided to proceed to Granbury and have lunch there, about 50 miles farther. Still the wind was pounding but we made good time. Jill pulled into Braum's. It was an excellent choice, quick and cheap. We were famished and thirsty. It was hard work riding a motorcycle in a wind tunnel. People get hungry. After wolfing down a couple of burgers and fries, we were back in the saddle.

We accumulated another 70 miles till we hit Comanche. This time it was the Bonnies that needed attention and a drink. We got good mileage out of the bikes—about 57 mpg. When we stopped at a Shell gas station, it started to warm up a little. We treated ourselves to coffee and some Subway cookies. Zeb made another pit stop and gladly stretched his legs. The little guy was the perfect backseater.

Time was of the essence. Loafing around in the morning and the stops, necessary or not, had burned up too much daylight. We knew we had to make up time. The pressure was on to get to our destination before nightfall.

Gary and Connie's cabin was in unfamiliar country, away from population and nearly impossible to find in the dark. No room for error. And then there is Murphy's law. We were supposed to hit I-16 near Goldthwaite but missed it. It was partially my fault. I noticed the sign but was over-confident that Jill had seen it too and knew what she was doing. Apparently her radar was switched off at that particular moment, and we both passed it. About five miles outside Goldthwaite, she realized something was not right and pulled over. When I told her I had seen a sign at the town's intersection and not bothered to make her aware of it, I was so glad she wasn't carrying a baseball bat!

We had to backtrack the five miles to town and start over. Llano was still 55 miles away, and it was already 4:15 p.m. Dusk was setting in and on top of that it looked like it was going to rain. Dark, heavy clouds hovered over the Llano region. Temperatures dropped tremendously, and the wind was picking up again.

Miraculously, the weather gods were on our side, and the threatening storm subsided just as fast as it appeared.

At 5:30 p.m., after some of the most sublime maneuverings by my lovely leader through little unknown back roads, we arrived at the gate. A push on the button and it opened like an inviting arm. About 50 feet of pressed gravel took us to our friends' garage. I put my kick stand down but quickly realized that this thin metal rod was no match on gravel. We decided to park on the concrete slab in front of their garage, Jill on the right, me on the left. I looked at my wife and saw the outline of her sunglasses on her wind beaten, reddish tired face. But, there was still enough energy left for a smile. She had become an instant pro.

We had about 15 minutes of daylight left to pick out a spot and set up shop. Our friends were nowhere to be seen—probably on an errand. We walked around the premises and threw our bags down about 20 yards to the side of their cabin. This spot was going to be home for two days.

Gary told me that everything on his property either prickles or bites and how right he was. There were flora and fauna of the worst kind: cacti, ants, and stickers. Everything nipped or punctured us. We made a little clearing and by the end of the day we hadn't done too badly. We planted ourselves in folding chairs and nourished our insides with cheese and crackers we had stuffed in our bags at the last moment. We were too tired to get out and find a place to eat.

Coffee never tasted so good as we sat there in the quietness of the evening (except for the noises of crickets, quails, birds, frogs, dogs and some other critters I'm afraid to think about). But the presence of Jill made it all good and wonderful. This trip was already worth it even if it should rain for the next two days.

Darkness arrived without further notice, and so did our friends who returned from a trip to historic Fredericksburg. It was 7:30 p.m. by then and we told them we were going to take a quick nap and join them later. Well, we woke up two hours later! Our batteries were 30 percent charged, enough to get up and walk to the cabin. Gary and Connie offered us some left over pizza, and we gobbled it down like two hungry wolves.

We chit-chatted awhile about the day's passage and promised our hosts that we would serve them bacon and eggs in the morning, cowboy style.

We staggered back to the tent and crawled into our sleeping bags without further ado.

"Good night Ma," I said.

"Good night Pa," she returned.

The night went by and was alright, I guess (except for the feeling of having spent eight hours like a corpse on a marble slab). I wanted to go in all Rambo and use my old army mat to buffer the hardness of the ground, but it didn't pan out that way. Guess age crept into my bones. Yeah, my airborne days are surely over. Comfort is now the name of the game.

On my right side was my dear spouse all duffled up in her sleeping bag with only one eye visible, probably the one she opens when there is an alarm situation. She looked pretty comfortable on her blow-up mattress—another mistake I wouldn't make again.

Zeb woke up too but, although I wanted to strangle him for most of the night, he did quite well. He heard noises that were there, but also ones that weren't and his constant growling drove me to the point of insanity. I unzipped the front opening of the tent and let him out.

It was sunny but cool. I crawled out and took a towel. I was going to freshen up at the cold water spigot—man vs. nature.

Barechested and full of confidence, I strode to the spot where the water well was located. Meanwhile, Gary came out to raise his flag.

I turned on the water and cupped some in my hands. It was very cold and smelled like wet rusty iron. With a small public watching, there was no way I could retreat. I had to go through with it and make a damn fool of myself. I threw some water over my back and tried vigorously not to flinch. I'm sure there were some jealous looks (or not) but all I wanted to do was to take off and sit in the sun for 30 seconds. I walked away like a caveman with frozen nipples but with his head held high. Now it was time for BACON.

We brought eggs and bacon on the trip, and cooked those on the two small burners we packed. These things worked like a charm. In no time, Jill had results, and the smell of bacon and eggs filled the Llano air.

Gary and Connie came over, and we all filled our plates. Then and there I knew life could be simple. You only had to accept it. I could do this forever and be happy. I felt fulfillment at that moment. I was lucky to finally have found someone to share this with. I realized I didn't need much after all. Our friends had it right. This was a wonderful place. Heaven sometimes is hidden in small corners.

It promised to be a glorious day, so Jill and I were eager to go out and explore the area. We decided to shed our leathers and wear light jackets since it was only a short ride. Gary told us there was not much "going on" in downtown Llano, but it was still worth visiting. He was right.

Llano was a one-street town with one intersection, but quite picturesque. Still you got the impression that the landscape was changing, and life was becoming more laid back—definitely worth the exit on the interstate. Hunting season had just started, and camouflage was in fashion! We needed some supplies and stopped at the Dollar store, the place to be in Llano if you needed something essential, like Oil of Olay.

After that, we parked our bikes on the only side street Llano had to offer and strolled to the bridge over the Llano river (that, by itself, was worth doing). The water was pretty low, but it gave us the opportunity to see the river bed filled with heavy boulders. We crossed the bridge to look at a couple of antique shops and talked ourselves into descending the bank of the river and taking some pictures there. We sat down for a moment and took it all in. For about 30 minutes, we let the world go by—a wonderful feeling, not being noticed.

We got back in time to our bivouac and freshened up a little to go out again. This time we would ride with Gary and Connie. Zeb had to stay behind. Although our friends' property was fenced, we didn't want Zeb to roam loose, so we tied him to a tree with a 30 foot leash (for Humane Society readers). Still, I didn't like it but he should be OK. That morning he made friends with three neighboring dogs and the chance he would take off was iffy—too far from home to take risks.

Back to Llano we went. Gary pointed out a few things we should investigate on our next trip down and gave a few tips. We already decided earlier to come back in the spring. We liked it here, away from the stress of everyday life—a good place to hide.

We stopped at a Mexican restaurant. The food wasn't all that great, but I think, for the most part, we were too tired to eat. After that, we returned to their cabin, only stopping to get a bag of marshmallows.

At the tent site, Zeb was nowhere to be seen! Just when panic was about to set in, he came running out of the brush, his stubby tail wagging. Still in shock or maybe more mortified, I walked over to the tree where I had tied him up. He simply got his head out of his collar. From the evidence he left behind, I could see that it didn't take him all that long either. We resolved to take him with us in the future.

Before we left for dinner, I had gathered up rocks to make a circle and piled up some dry wood to make a campfire. Luckily the county burn ban had been lifted, and we could go ahead and make a fire. In my book, you can't go camping without setting fire to something. I got my brand new miniature ax from my saddle bag and started chopping. Now was the time to become a frontier mountain man. When I got finished, I wanted to smell like one. To the others I must have looked no more than a little kid playing in a sandbox but the vigor I produced by my hacking kept them silent. Or maybe they felt sorry for me. I will never know, and that's a good thing.

I cut some sticks to roast the marshmallows and was ready to start the pyrotechnics. The kindling caught fire with no problems and in less than a minute, I had a good blaze going.

The four of us sat there under a bright starry sky gazing at the fire for almost four hours, drinking Sangria and munching marshmallows. Marshmallows are wasted on me. All I got out of them was a lot of gagging and a sticky beard—a blemish on my Jeremiah Johnson image. Sometimes I just don't get the "American Way." S'mores are awful.

Suddenly the Llano night silence was disrupted by Connie's scream to look up. And there, just for a fraction of a second, was the biggest meteor I had ever seen, splitting up before our eyes! It was a present from the heavens and a nice ending to a wonderful evening.

We each had a cup of coffee, brewed on our stove, to end the day, and as all outlaws do, I poured the rest of the coffee over the coals so we wouldn't be detected or scalped by Indians when we bedded down. We exchanged good-nights with our friends and crawled one more time in our wickiup.

Thinking things were bad for me the first night, it was now worse because I knew what was coming. At home, Zeb goes through a nest-building ritual where he steps in the middle of his blanket and works it with all fours. I'm telling you that in a confined space, this just does not work with humans around. I decided to lay down and take it like a man. Meanwhile, Jill, nice and cozy cocooned in her sleeping bag, enjoyed the comfort of not being stupid. After 15 minutes of tossing and turning, I gave up and assumed the position for the night. I still regret that night's sleep to this very day. Something in my neck must have fused together that night—I still feel it.

Well, all good things come to an end, as did our trip. But we had loved it, and if we could make it home without trouble, the roads were ours from then on.

Jill started to break down camp while I contained my morning cold shower at the spigot to just brushing my teeth. Good enough.

I started re-packing the Bonnevilles and again it went like I had been doing it all my life. So within the hour we were ready to go. Glad to go home but sad it was over. Time had flown. But both of us felt replenished with another experience and the satisfaction that it was only the beginning of our travels.

We hugged Gary and Connie, said our goodbyes and thanked them again for their hospitality. Gary took one last picture of the three members of the 50/50 Motorcycle Club and opened the gate to let us through.

We headed back the same way we'd come. The goal was again to get home before dark, and we were already more than one hour ahead of schedule. After 35 miles, we stopped to fuel up in San Saba, a small town between Comanche and Llano. We pulled up at the local gas station and parked our bikes in front of one of the pumps. At the same time, an old beat-up pick-up truck parked on the opposite side of the pump. The door swung open, and a rough looking old-timer nodded at me with a straight weathered face and disappeared inside the small convenience store. A minute later he was back, coming straight at me.

"Hey buddy, I seen the mutt on the back of your motor-sickle. How long it took ya to teach him that?" he said.

"Zeb is pretty smart. It didn't take me much time at all to teach him," I explained.

"Well," he continued, "On the farm I got me an old New Zealand heeler and he rides in the back of the truck. You know how I taught him to stay in there?"

Looking at the Neanderthal in front of me, I was almost afraid to ask, but I finally did.

Politely, I asked, "Tell me."

"Well see, I put a chain around his neck, see, and hooked one end to the truck bed, and drove around the yard. When he jumped off, I let him hang there a little bit and choke a little bit see and from then on he stayed put," he said.

I swallowed painfully and nodded wisely with my hand rubbing my beard like he gave me the best advice ever. I could barely make myself respond but said, "Well, that's one way to do it, I guess."

"Well buddy, you and the misses have a great day," he said in parting. And as though he were on a secret mission, he got back in his truck and took off. I looked at Jill, and she looked at me, both without blinking an eye. The world is a strange place.

From there, we pushed on until we reached Dublin and made a stop there to have a root beer float. We parked in front of the restaurant and walked into an almost empty dining room area. However, five minutes later the place was packed with church goers. We didn't arrive a minute too soon. We could see through the window that Zeb was getting all the attention as cameras flashed. He had jumped back on my bike, looking like he owned it!

The weather was great but still windy, although not as bad as when we came down. We mounted our iron-horses and took off. This was going to be the longest stretch of the trip without a pit stop. The roads were fantastic, and slowly we could see the landscape go back to a more familiar shape.

Dublin, the home of Dr. Pepper, came in our sights and so did the craving for root beer and ice cream. Out of all places during our trip this little town outside Stephenville had the only traffic jam! How ironic. Luckily, we avoided the jam by a quick right-hand turn into the parking spots in front of the Dr. Pepper museum.

Unfortunately, we didn't have the time to visit the museum. But we did pick up a few souvenirs and T-shirts and treated ourselves to the long craved root beer float. They made it all from scratch including a couple of scoops of Blue Bell Vanilla—there are no words.

The last stretch was the hardest. We were tired and wanted to hang out on the couch ASAP. Traffic was almost nonexistent until we hit I-20. There, we were back, smack dab in the middle of it—and more wind joined into the mix.

Meanwhile Jill—without a worry in the world—was zooming the interstate at 75 mph, one hand on the throttle and the other scratching her nose and pushing her helmet down. I felt Zeb's teeth in my back trying to stay in his seat and me clutching the handlebars, holding on for dear life. That girl knows how to enjoy and use her windscreen to the fullest. Sure I looked cool without a shield, if only in the reflection of a window or at a stop sign, but at 80 mph and 30 knots headwind, it's a different story. Jill slowed down after a while, and when we pulled off one more time to get gas, I asked her if she could go any faster. She just grinned and—

with her wide open big brown eyes—said, "I was just trying to make up time."

Finally, Marsh Lane and the last few miles to a warm shower and feet-up were close at hand. It was a great ride to Llano, and we both loved every minute of it.

Marrying Jill was the best thing that ever happened to me, and I'm glad we're doing motorcycle touring together. I think we both want to continue to have adventures on our motorcycles and have more tales to tell.

—Jef Verswyvel

44. My Get-Off Got Me Riding

Back when I was young and stupid—not too long ago—I wanted one of those plastic slant bikes. Of course, mother wouldn't have it. Every time I almost had her talked into it, we'd see a wreck, which then shot my dreams to pieces.

When I was 17, I had a chance to crawl up on an R1—you see where this is going. I had never even ridden a dirt bike my whole life, let alone a 1000cc machine. A buddy had bought it and didn't know how to ride. A few other friends were showing him. Everyone was taking turns riding, and I showed up at the wrong time. A helmet got tossed into my hands, and the owner of the bike said, "Go for it."

I thought, "My soon-to-be wife is already pregnant, and we're getting married come November and this will be my only chance to ride a bike." So I jumped on it, fired it up, and barely touched the throttle when the RPM went out of control.

171

At that moment, something said GET OFF, but my pride grabbed the clutch and I took off. I probably didn't make it out of third gear. I was just pacing, thinking, "This is amazing!"

I went to the end of the street, stopped, and turned around. I had just shifted to second when I thought to put the visor down, which had been up the whole time. I reached up with my left hand to drop it down. With my right hand still on the throttle, I felt the bike jump up like a bull. It stood straight up as my back slammed onto the hot pavement, and the peg grabbed my pant leg.

The bike dragged me a few feet while the throttle was stuck open. The bike fell back on top of me, veered to the left, and started flipping. After the third flip, the bike let go of my pants with a rip and slung me toward a tree.

While in mid-flight, I saw the bike still flipping. All I could think was, "Oh shit, that's not my bike." I slammed against a tree with my lower tailbone and back, and then blacked out. I woke up to some guy smacking my helmet, telling me to wake up. He had been mowing his yard and saw it all happen. He asked if I needed an ambulance to which I replied "No, it's not my bike." It was the wrong thing to say, because he didn't call an ambulance, instead, the police.

The guys who were riding the bike before me, heard it happen and took off running my way. The owner of the bike didn't move.

Once the police showed up, I was taken to a hospital where they treated road rash all up my arms, back, hands, and yes, my ass. I had two cracked ribs, three fractures in my tailbone, and a slipped disk.

My mother was called and showed up at the hospital with my soon-to-be wife. Believe me, the straps they had me in on the backboard wouldn't break. I tried. I wasn't sure who to fear more: the police officer, my mother, or my pregnant fiancée.

I also called the owner of the bike pleading that I would pay him every last cent for that bike, and I did. $4,000 later he had another bike. I sold one of my two cars to get him the money, but I did nonetheless.

For months I was laid up on the couch getting the same earful each day: "Bet you don't want a bike now." After four months of hearing that, I had enough.

My wife and mother were sitting with me, and as I went to get up, I let out a moan and they snickered and said, "Bet you don't want a bike now."

But, I replied, "Oh yes I do, and I'll have one. Just wait and see."

Then, I bought my 1976 Bobber.

—Voodoo

45. How I Got Back Into Motorcycling

Four years ago, I was working 60 miles south of home. Daily commutes were approximately 125 miles. Then, high gas prices hit. A major portion of my budget was going in the tank instead of in my pocket. To reduce the strain on my budget, I decided to buy a motorcycle.

I read all the literature to find the best beginner's motorcycle. I had previous experience on trail bikes and one street bike, but I had not ridden a street bike in over 25 years. I felt inexperienced and that I needed to take the Motorcycle Safety Foundation (MSF) course to learn to ride safely. Then I would buy a small motorcycle.

I read numerous reviews of starter motorcycles, and went to dealers to look at the various recommended models. I was never in the market for a "sport" bike. I knew that a high center of gravity, short wheelbase, and power and speed were dangerous for a beginner. The Rebel 250 was too small. The Suzuki GZ250 was OK, but also felt small. Then I read reviews for the Virago 250. It didn't look or feel small like the other 250s, and its V-twin seemed to perform (and sound) better.

I found a used Virago 250 in a town about 100 miles south. But on the day I was to pick it up, a friend with a truck was not available. So I had my wife drive me down there, and I rode the bike back home. Believe me, it was scary doing this after not riding for almost 25 years. But, my co-pilot was right behind me, working as a blocker. The ride home was uneventful.

The Virago 250 was an immaculate 2006, with 4000 miles. Everyone liked it, most thought it was a bigger motorcycle. I didn't have any trouble riding the first two to three weeks, staying local and south of town on country roads. However, I got overconfident and decided to give my wife a ride. On the way home, I hit a water bottle in a driveway and almost dropped the bike. Of course, this scared the crap out of my wife. Since then, she has never ridden with me.

I passed the local learners written test and was going to take the driving portion of the test, when something unusual happened. The DMV decided to re-paint the markings on the parking lot where they gave the driving test. So, they extended my learners permit for three months until the lot was painted, and they let me practice on the course anytime I wanted. They even left the cones out over the weekend so I could practice! This was a big advantage in my re-learning how to ride, since I had decided not to take the MSF course—bad idea. But I had safe practice areas in the country and the DMV parking lot.

I passed the driving portion of the course three months later (on my Virago 250). I rode that little Virago as often as possible over the next two years, some expressway, some back roads, and almost every day to work. I had close calls and some learning experiences, but overall, it was a great motorcycle on which to train.

After two years on the Virago (and over 25,000 miles), I was looking to move up, but the engine on my wife's car went out. The only available down payment was my little Virago. The dealer was interested in it, and several salesmen tested it in the parking lot. The salesmen all said that if I didn't trade it for a car, they would buy it outright. I parted with my little Virago and drove away in a nice car for my wife (how many guys would do that?).

My wife agreed that since I used my Virago to buy a car for her, the next time gas prices went up (and I had a bonus), I could get another motorcycle. That happened early this year. So I started the search again for a replacement motorcycle.

My bonus came in, but was less than anticipated. I had a limited budget, and a short time to buy. My search sent me in the direction of the Shadow VLX. Oddly enough, it is considered a beginner motorcycle to some. And others complain about the 4-speed transmission. An older VLX not only fit my budget, it was a very practical "next step."

I found a 1997 VLX in average shape (very rusted) with a perfect engine. The owner had taken the Japanese motorcycle repair course and was using this bike on which to practice. The engine had been tuned, the carbs re-jetted, and aftermarket pipes installed. Complaints about the 4-speed seemed to be unfounded (different sprocket?).

This bike ran on the expressway with no problems. It had been stored in a barn for several years, and was quite dirty. I spent several weeks getting most of the rust off and cleaning up the bike.

Then, it looked great. I got compliments everywhere I went. It was a VLX 600CD, two-tone red and pearl.

However, the purchase of a "new" bike caught the attention of my co-worker. He then began research on purchasing a bike of his own. Gas prices were affecting his budget also, but he decided to take a different path than I took. He settled on a 400cc Yamaha Majesty scooter. Like me, he had not ridden a motorcycle in over 25 years, so he should have considered himself a beginner. But, he owned a Honda 750 four back in the seventies, so he thought he could handle a scooter.

I recommended the local MSF course, and told him how I had an advantage when re-learning to ride several years ago. He decided to buy the scooter and learned on his own.

The first week, he dropped his scooter in his garage. He went in too fast, hit the rail that holds the garage door, and tore off the exhaust cover. He dropped it on the left side with only minor scratches. The second week, he hit a piece of Styrofoam™ when turning into a parking lot, and dropped the scooter again. This time the damage was more severe (also on the left side). I brought him a can of matching spray paint to cover up the damage.

We planned a ride two weeks later, and my co-worker had plotted out a circular course that would be entertaining. But he never showed up, so I went on and visited my parents. I called him when I got home, and as it turned out, he had another accident. He had decided to take his driving test that morning, and stopped by the DMV. However, during the emergency lane-change and stop maneuver, he over-applied the front brakes and flipped. He broke his collarbone and several ribs. He was out of work three weeks. I don't know what the future of his riding will be or if he will sell his bike or not.

No matter how much flak I may have received about buying a small bike to learn on, I have never regretted it. It turned out to be the best decision I have ever made. I put over 25,000 miles on that Virago. In the early '80s, I put about 3,000 miles on a small Harley (Aermacchi 350). And now, I have put over 2,000 miles on my VLX. That adds up to almost 30,000 miles.

I don't want to jinx myself here and make a statement. I just thought that another beginner might read this, and decide not to buy a big sport bike or cruiser at the beginning of their motorcycle career. That decision just might save his or her life.

—Kevin Mowen

46. 24 Hours

It was all quite a simple plan really. I have two friends that, for the sake of this tale we'll call Nikki and Sam. It was Nikki's twenty-first birthday, and we were going to drive—them in the car, me on my KLR—from below sea level in Norfolk, 300 miles to the highest town in England, Princetown in Devon (Nikki's hometown), for her party. Unbeknownst to her, Sam was also going to propose to her.

We set off at around one in the morning. For around half an hour we drove down familiar, flat Norfolk roads, making good time. The only vehicles on the road were random lorries on late night hauls. We had covered about 30 miles before we hit the first problem of the trip.

Coming off a roundabout, I pulled the clutch in to change up a gear, only for the clutch lever to flop helplessly in my hand. I flashed my lights and pulled to the side of the road. This could not have just happened—but it did.

Sam turned his car around and came back to see what the problem was. Where the clutch cable connected to the engine, the end had snapped off. For a good ten minutes, we tried and tried to tie the cable round, but to no avail.

A police car stopped to see what had happened and drove off after I told them I didn't have breakdown coverage. So I formed a plan. I'd try to ride the poor, clutchless bike back home while Sam carried on, up to Devon. I would then see if I could pinch a clutch cable off one of my other bikes. With some convincing, Sam agreed, and I set off on my return journey.

Setting off was hard with the front wheel lifting every time I dropped her into first. Stopping was even harder, crunching between first and second until I found neutral. I tried to drive in sixth gear as much as possible, only changing down if I needed to.

Annoyingly, every lorry I met on the way back pulled over to let me pass, seemingly thinking that the biker behind them was getting annoyed with their 40 mph pace.

Eventually, I got back home and after 15 minutes to remove the exhaust—annoyingly, in the way of the cable—the cable was off, and although ill-fitting, bodged onto the KLR. Filled with joy, I hopped back onto the KLR and set off again, this time on my own.

The KLR and I rode happily for hours from Norfolk to Cambridge and onto our first motorway, the M11. Happy to be making good progress and overtaking the late night lorries, we drove on until we were near the beginning of the M25 and stopped for petrol and a break for the KLR and a cigarette and an energy drink for me.

I spoke to Sam on the phone. They'd taken a different route and got lost due to diversions trying to get onto the M5. At this point, I couldn't even have imagined what lay ahead of me.

We set off again and got onto the M25. I drove for hours and hours, and the calm nighttime turned into a hectic morning with the sun blinding me as it rose on the Motorway. 100 miles passed. Surely, I should have seen the exit by now?

I drove and drove praying to see a sign for the M5. Eventually, I admitted to myself that I was lost on London's ring road. The KLR was unhappy too, a faint but noticeable ticking noise developing. I decided to stop again, and call Sam to see if he could find me some directions. But, coming off the motorway into a service station, with a lorry in the left lane ahead of me and a car in my lane ahead of me, I once again felt a lever flop to the handlebar, but this time it wasn't the clutch.

I had no choice. I twisted open the throttle and shot between the two vehicles, gritting my teeth. With the car ahead braking to slow down from 70, there was no chance of me not hitting into the back of him on the rear drum brake alone. Luckily, I got through and, heart racing, I pulled to the side of the road to see what had happened.

The brake caliper was dangling by the brake line. The bolts had vibrated completely out and were nowhere to be seen. I pushed my poor KLR up to the service station's car park and phoned Sam. (By then I'd been awake for almost 24 hours and driving for at least nine.)

He had no idea what to do either. His only suggestion was to ask people with vans or trailers to take me and my bike. It was a typically horrible service station, infested with ants, but, unfortunately, I had to spend a large amount of time inside charging my phone. Eventually, hours later, my dad (God bless him) agreed to drive all the way down to bring me two bolts, brake fluid, and engine oil for my bike.

I passed the time talking to the bikers I saw driving in, who almost always stopped to see what the problem was. Even those on the most expensive bikes would scour over their bikes seeing if they had any bolts the same they could safely remove from their bikes to donate to me.

I did try to sleep, but with the motorway beside you, it's a lot easier said than done. The happiness I felt when I saw my dad's battered Nissan Micra pulling in was unbelievable. After we had a good chat, got the KLR topped off on oil, and fastened the caliper firmly on with an impact driver and hammer, we set off on our separate ways, and I went back onto the M25.

Now you'd think that this would have been enough problems for one journey, but no. You see, there never was an exit for the M5 on the M25. I was confused. I thought I took the M5 to the M4, but it's the other way around, and not knowing this, I set off on the M25 once again looking for the M5.

Hours and hundreds of miles later, I thought I'd take a chance and set off down the M4. It's a good thing I did, or I might well still have been on the M25 today.

I was so happy to see signs for SOUTHWEST, that I almost cried. I pulled into another service station a short way down the M4 to tell Sam the situation, only to find out that Nikki's party was now just hours away.

I jumped back on my KLR, kicked her to life, and shot off down the M4, doing seriously illegal speeds in an attempt to make up lost time—my latest mistake.

The M4 went by pretty uneventfully, but there was one thing I didn't take into account about my full throttle riding—fuel consumption. Now on the M5, the KLR made the horribly familiar noise of a bike that's out of petrol. I pulled onto the hard shoulder and went to flip the fuel to reserve (the first time I'd ever had to use reserve on this bike). No big problem, right? Right, except it already *was* set to reserve.

I pulled out my phone, texted Sam, and then my phone died. I was now sitting on the hard shoulder of the M5 with no phone and a bike that was out of petrol. I rolled a cigarette and cried.

I hadn't been there long when a motorway police car pulled onto the hard shoulder behind me. Luckily, these were not just *any* motorway cops. In a car, they may have been, but they were true bikers at heart. They took sympathy on me and together we shook the poor old KLR about, rustling up the last dregs of fuel and then pushed me down the hard shoulder to give me a bump start. Then the KLR fired up once more. I thanked them from the bottom of my heart and set off again hoping to hit a petrol station too, but I didn't even cover two miles before she died again.

Again the cops stopped and helped me bump start her, this time saying I could drive down the hard shoulder doing 20 mph, and they'd drive behind me with their lights on. So once again I set off, this time with a police escort. A couple of bump starts and a few miles later, still no petrol station and the KLR was completely dry.

Not many cops would ever have done as much as these had already done, but still they didn't stop helping. They helped push the KLR off the motorway behind a barrier so it couldn't be moved and gave me a lift up to the next petrol station (one off the motorway to save me money too!) to buy petrol in a can. Then, they gave me a lift all the way back.

They were the nicest cops I have ever met in my entire life. I'll never forget them. They stayed till the KLR was filled up with petrol and running once again, and once more I set off.

Think it's over yet? I would've thought that'd be my last problem. I hoped it would be, but there was one more problem for me.

Running the bike that low on fuel must've pulled all the crap sitting in my petrol tank through, as, near Bristol, I started noticing it was getting harder to do high speeds. The problem got progressively worse and worse, until with the bike struggling to keep at 60, I pulled into another service station.

From this point on my memory gets pretty hazy, as I had been awake for nearly two days. But I believe the bike would only rev high with choking and low without it. I gave her some Redex and set off again, stressed and upset. It took me hours to finish those last few miles of the M5, the KLR pulling 50 mph at the absolute maximum towards the end—downhill—but she never would completely die.

I stopped in almost every service station for coffee as I didn't have the mental power or willpower to carry on anymore. I was seriously upset. Freezing after such a long ride, I finally made it into Devon and off the M5. On the Devon Expressway I stopped for one more time, hope given up. I was cold. My visor was frosting up. My glasses were frosting up. My hands were numb. How had my life come to this? I eventually managed to gather the willpower to cover those last few miles off the Devon Expressway and into the (oh so beautiful, oh so fun) roads of Dartmoor.

I flipped on the choke every time I needed to climb a hill, and took it off as soon as I got to the top for compression braking, otherwise I'd shoot off like a rocket (23% gradients is a normal hill where I was).

Eventually, I made it into Princetown at 1:30 in the morning. It'd been more than 24 hours on the road and even longer I'd been awake. I missed the party, missed them getting engaged, and sadly I had more problems with the KLR and ended up having to sell it while I was there. The bike, from which I took the clutch cable, also got stolen while I was in Princetown.

I now own a CB500. It's taken me on the same journey there AND back with no problems, but it's such a boring ride, it's unbelievable. I'd take the KLR any day and, hopefully, one of these days, I'll be able to afford a KLR600.

—Hippy Vince

47. Drifting in France

I got married on 29 October 2004, in Macon, Georgia. This date was hastily chosen because it was the last good weekend to profit from the wonderful colors of the autumn leaves. My French bride, Martine, a newcomer to the motorcycling world, was excited about the idea of going on our honeymoon on a motorcycle. After a simple wedding ceremony in the company of good friends, we took off on our pristine Virago 1100 for a wonderful week drifting in the Appalachian Mountains. After that happy adventure, we vowed always to go on a motorcycle ride for our anniversary.

Since we arrived in France, four years ago, we only managed one-day token rides on this date. We did have fun riding the lower Alps, exploring the northern coast of Brittany, and last year, hunting castles in the Loire valley, where we now live, but this time we were going to try to repeat our first ride.

We had a little over a week off, and my wife wanted to see a region of her country called the Black Perigord. This area is located about 100 miles east of Bordeaux. It forms part of a group of Perigords: the green, the white, the purple and the black.

The black area is a popular tourist destination because of the nice little medieval villages that lay along the river Dordogne, each one with its own medieval castle. There are also some prehistoric troglodyte settlements, so I was sure to *feel at home* there.

I had just sold my Triumph Trophy and bought a Virago 1100 of the same year as the one we rode when we got married. I insisted on "drifting." You just take off and "go that way" without worrying about schedules, places to be, or things to do. The only thing we had to consider was the weather, as it had been a dreadful year in that department.

No worries about packing either. I announced that we would put everything into my green U.S. Army duffel bag and strap it to the sissy bar with bungee cords, just like hippie bikers of the '60s used to do.

The weekend came, but we couldn't leave, at least not on a motorcycle. It was raining. In fact, it had been raining for two weeks. I convinced my wife to wait till Monday morning as the weather gurus promised an improvement.

Sunday afternoon I decided to pack the bike to see how that went. I put most of our stuff into the duffel bag and strapped it to the sissy bar. Then I realized this idea was not going to work. The bag sagged and covered the tail light. Besides, it didn't look as cool as in the biker movies of the '60s. I was starting to panic.

I didn't have saddle bags, and if I couldn't find a way to pack all this, we'd be going by car, an idea that my wife started to consider more and more as the weekend passed. But providence stepped in and saved the day.

I spied a piece of luggage in the corner of the garage, one of those carry-on bags with wheels and an extendable handle, the ones everyone drags around at the airport. It just so happened to have a sleeve that would fit perfectly over the sissy bar, if I removed the handle and wheels, thereby ruining it.

Luckily, my wife had gone to take "El Gato," the fat lazy old cat, to the cat sitter. Out came the drill and in no time the frame was off. The bag easily slid over the sissy bar. The trip was still on.

That evening, kneeling on the living room carpet, my wife and I packed the bag with the excitement of two kids going to summer camp. That same night, I mounted the bag on the bike. I added a small rolled towel to keep it from rubbing on the fender, covered the whole thing with a trash bag, and secured it with two bungee cords. The system was neat and waterproof, and I could hold my gloves and scarf on the bungees. The only problem was that we had been downgraded from hippie bikers to plain riff-raff.

Monday morning we got up without hurry—unlike other rides where I stressed before leaving. This time I didn't care. We're drifting, so what if we left at eleven in the morning—no worries.

Despite the gloomy weather, I was upbeat. I decided that the GPS and the maps could stay at home. All I needed to know was that I was going to Bordeaux, then turn left on the A-89 and wait for the sign to Sarlat la Caneda.

I opened the garage door and pushed the bike out. The farmland was covered with a thick, wet fog. I couldn't see very far. I observed the scenery as the bike warmed up. It felt like a biplane was preparing to take off on a gloomy morning during World War I.

My wife appeared. She was smiling under her helmet. We mounted the bike and were off. What made a couple approaching their fiftieth birthdays want to get on a motorcycle on a day like this? It was cold, miserable, and foggy. There was mud on the road from the tractors, and it was so humid that it was almost like rain, yet we were happy to be on the road on a motorcycle.

I think it is the perspective. Yes, traveling by car is like riding in a submarine, protected by fathomless obscurity of comfort. One relaxes in the boredom of the sealed perspective, where surface woes can hardly bother the mind, entertained by distant voices coming from the antenna and quick looks through the tinted glass of the periscope, now and then "surfacing" at a gas station or rest area for a whiff of clean air and a quick look at the scenery.

Like "surface skimmers," we find ourselves at the mercy of the weather. We sit behind our handlebars grinning under blue skies, or clenching our teeth in determination when heavy rain hits us square in the face. And only under untenable circumstances, do we seek refuge on the leeward side of a motel's parking lot or under any convenient portico.

In exchange, we get to be at one with nature, making the arrival to our destination an almost spiritual experience. That's why you will find us, port side, in a cozy corner of our favorite hangout, exchanging stories of past voyages, eventually putting some on paper in an attempt to share them with our distant motorcycle brothers and sisters. Yes, I think it is all about perspective.

I steered carefully around the runabouts. It was slippery, and I couldn't see much. Slowly, we left behind the familiar farmland and entered the highway. I love highways, trouble free traveling, good gas stations, efficient cruising speeds and here in France, immaculate road surfaces. But it comes at a cost.

You have to pay tolls on almost every highway. Another big difference from the U.S. is that there's no advertising on the road. The only things you see are road signs and signs telling you how far the nearest gas stations are, and how much the fuel costs. You can watch the scenery and relax without being bombarded by advertising. The only problem is that you have no idea where the next hotel is unless you did your homework before leaving, or you know the area.

After paying the toll at the exit of the Nantes bypass, we were heading south on A-83, trying to settle in for a long trip. We traveled in a halo of 400 yards. You couldn't see anything beyond that. It was so humid, that my helmet visor was wet like in the rain. I could feel humidity penetrating my leathers as I stubbornly refused to wear a rain suit—after all, it was going to get better, no?

After a while, conditions worsened. I should have stopped and put on the suits, but I didn't. That would mean defeat, submission to the weather, and so I dangerously continued to roll the dice knowing full well what happens when leathers get soaked.

Visibility was down to 150 yards, so I took refuge behind a truck. Here, trucks are not as fast as in the U.S. They are governed to 60 mph, so there's not much turbulence behind them. This one was from Poland. We followed him for a few miles then I gave up, and pulled into the next gas station, as we needed fuel and food.

We had a quick, hot meal. My wife was in a good mood, but there was a gloomy feeling lingering over the possibility of spending the next week in this weather.

Back on the highway all was well. The weather was improving. One hour later, we reached Niort, and I pulled into a gas station before we changed to the A-10 toward Bordeaux. It was a Leclerc station—nice—even had a living room inside. I quickly settled into the couch to enjoy a cup of coffee. My wife was looking at a map on the wall and called me over. She was worried about arriving at Bordeaux at peak hour and getting stuck in traffic on the bypass. She pointed to a shortcut passing through Angouleme. I hesitated. Most secondary roads were slow-going here. There was a village every 10 miles with runabouts, stop lights, mobile chicanes, tractors, semis, old guys in Renaults, etc. I studied the map once more and then decided we would stick to the original plan.

Back outside, things were looking up, and off we went, following the green signs that said "Bordeaux." Another hour of uneventful highway travel and I saw a sign: "Cognac, Angouleme." Without even thinking, I took the exit, the shortcut my wife spoke about, and soon we're doing 40 mph behind a truck.

The near sunny afternoon, great scenery, and even passing through Cognac—the famous town where all the big brands were—could not make up for the fact that we were advancing at the pace of a sailboat, impossible to arrive in Sarlat by the end of the day. The torture continued for the rest of the afternoon, and just as the sun settled, low on fuel, we arrived at Angouleme, without any idea where we were going to sleep.

I followed the signs to downtown, looking for a cafe. Like many towns around here, this one had a very old center area, surrounded by more modern suburbs complete with malls and supermarkets. It could have been the ancestral home for the Addams family—what a gloomy dark city!

As we reached the center, located on top of a steep hill, we stopped to look at a statue and take some photos, and then we continued traveling on narrow gray streets surrounded by old macabre building fronts covered with moss. It looked like a city of vampires. We ended up on a small square with a big menacing looking building on one side and a cafe on the other. I parked next to some scooters.

A hot cup of coffee and a delicious piece of cake made me feel much better. We asked the lady behind the counter about hotels. She explained that there were lots around, but the closest was just 200 yards away—nice, old, and with "charm."

Soon after, we re-mounted the bike and went looking. Two blocks away we found a small plaza with a fountain, and then the hotel. I parked in front and stayed with the bike while my wife went in to check. We were only going to stay there if there was a garage for the bike. I didn't want the vampires messing with my ride in the middle of the night.

Fifteen minutes later, she came out followed by a smiling, well-dressed man, like the concierges in the horror movies. They motioned to follow, so I fired up the machine and followed them 50 yards to the garage, where he let me park next to his boss's car, a place of honor I guess. I removed the bag, and we went inside.

"No way in hell," I said when I saw the inside. "I'm not sleeping here. Look at this place. It's full of ghosts."

The old hotel had been renovated, surely the project of someone's enthusiastic and affluent wife. The walls were deep red, the stairs, and its intricate iron work were purple. Incredibly, there was a modern elevator. On the second floor, we entered the dark corridor—more like a vaulted ceiling tunnel—and found a very old wooden door leading to our room.

Inside, the surprises continued. The whole room was painted in a deep peach color, including even the ancient iron radiator that dutifully continued to heat the room. "Is this to keep the ghosts away?" I commented. "Only doofuses like us would sleep in a room this color."

The next morning we went down for breakfast. I decided to try the stairs. They were so old, that the steps creaked and sagged under my weight. I tried to imagine how many people had already passed through here, and what it must have been like 100 years ago.

Then we came to a fabulous red room, with heavy red curtains, red table tops, red window frames, and a very old wooden floor. I could not get over this room. It looked like something out of *The Shining*. We calmly enjoyed our breakfast, relaxing in another world and then we left to get the bike. No more ghosts for us!

As we saddled up at the next gas station I told my wife, "First cafe with tables on the sidewalk, I'll stop." 70 miles later I was still looking for one. I couldn't believe it. We passed at least eight villages, and there was no cafe open. Of course, we knew that if we left the main road and went to the next village's church, we were sure to find one. There was always an open cafe in front of any church.

We arrived at the A-89 highway where we pulled into a big modern gas station just in time to have lunch. We had a good meal in the well-stocked cafeteria, rested, and then got back on the road. We had only about 50 miles to go. The sun was shining, and the road was great. We could feel we were out of the "dark ages" and into tourist-land.

We rode happily and slowly, enjoying the first sunny day in more than two weeks. After some time, we came upon a small picnic area on the side of the road. It was located next to an old railroad bridge with big arches, like a viaduct. We parked, and lay down on the picnic tables that were soaking up the sun. It felt great staring up into the sky and listening to the breeze in the leaves, with not a worry in our lives. "This is where the vacation starts," I said.

We took some pictures and then continued on, soon arriving at Sarlat. We opted for the now familiar tactic: follow the signs to downtown [*Centre ville*] then to the tourist office. If you're ever lost in France, do this. There's a tourist office in almost every town. There you can get the help you need, in English.

As we arrived, we could see that this medieval town was spotless. Its buildings, made with tan/light peach colored stones, contributed to the pleasant feeling of a well-cared-for tourist town. The deeper we went, the narrower the streets became, until we cruised at 20 mph in second gear on cobblestone roads where businesses of all sorts awaited clients. We advanced with the rhythmic pulses of the engine reverberating on the ancient walls like a muffled drum call of an impending execution. It was pure pleasure. I was mesmerized. It was the first time I had seen anything like this.

Carefully steering around pedestrians, we arrived at the tourist office where a mountain of information awaited: maps, brochures, and lists of hotels and bed & breakfasts (*gites* in French). After a few calls, we decided on a *gite* close to us—a mere 200 yards— that offered secure parking for the bike, all this in the middle of a medieval town.

It was a mansion, with towers, and all, hidden behind a big stone wall. We were led up the tower's stairs into a big room with 7-foot windows, a fireplace, and some very old furniture, including a small table with a mirror, used by ladies to do their make-up, this one so old, it still had candle holders. The bathroom, equally big, had three 7-foot windows, a very old sink, a big bathtub, and a bidet, all with ancient brass fittings. There was no shower. "Only rich people took baths in those days," explained my wife.

200 yards away, lay the garage for the motorcycle. Once the bike was secured, we left to see the town.

Back at the *gite*, once I overcame the fear that someone might have committed suicide in it, I took a great, relaxing bath in the enormous bathtub.

After breakfast the next day, we got on the bike and followed a blacktop road that twisted through a forest then joined the river's edge, very similar to riding in the Appalachian Mountains early on an autumn morning. The fog had not yet lifted when we arrived in the sleepy medieval village where I stopped at a cafe to warm up a bit. Then we got back on the bike to take a look around, but we didn't get far.

The village was small, and most roads were for pedestrians or too steep for a motorcycle. Steep, that's the word. One thing you should learn by heart is that medieval castles were military installations, and as such, they built them in nearly inaccessible areas, this one on top of a steep hill next to the river. I was puffing and panting as I went up carrying my helmet and wondered how they managed to carry all those stones up the hill to build the castle. The views got better and better as we climbed and as the fog lifted. There before us was the castle.

This castle was a war machine: Spartan, purposeful, cool as hell. Even the entrance to the kitchen had a drawbridge! The highest point for me was standing on the observation tower overlooking the valley, the river and the village. The view was breathtaking. There was a straight drop to the river—a long way down.

Back down at the river's bank, we prepared to leave for our next destination: La Roque Cageac, a mere seven miles away.

After a short, but picturesque, ride, we arrived. This village was on the list of most beautiful towns in France, and she certainly was beautiful, sitting at the bottom of a steep cliff right on the bank of a river, whose lazy waters reflected the scenery. Viewed from the right angle, it was a perfect postcard.

We were directed to see Domme. Getting there required a short climb up the mountain, riding on a steep, twisted, humid road that passed under the canopies of big trees. Back into the sunlight, we arrived at one of the entrances of the fortified village. This was a small medieval village encircled by a hefty defense wall with guard towers and heavy doors. Once inside, I rode to a scenic lookout. We enjoyed the view into the river valley, but I wanted to spend the last few hours of sunlight doing what I like the most: riding the motorcycle. Fortunately, Martine felt the same way, and as we saddled up, I proposed just to ride around without a destination in mind and see what happened. She answered, "Yes" with enthusiasm.

Back at the bottom of the mountain, we arrived at an intersection, and I asked if we should go left or right. "Left," came the muffled answer from under her helmet. Driving around aimlessly on the river valley's roads proved to be fun. The road signs meant nothing to us as we turned left or right guided only by instinct and the desire to have fun. I was zenning as we drifted in the sunny afternoon, passing through the virgin scene as we followed the road into a calm future.

Next morning at breakfast, the proprietor had bad news. An angry storm front was approaching from the sea. It would bring cold and freezing rain and be here this afternoon. Hunched over his computer, we observed the radar screen. Sure enough, the front was coming in, already reaching Bordeaux. It extended all the way to Brest. I studied the repeating movement of the screen. Not good. Going home the short way required heading to Bordeaux, where we'd meet the storm head on. Then we're sure to spend the rest of the trip under freezing rain.

So I borrowed a tactic from the sailing days: I squared off. I planned to set stern to the weather and move away from the storm, going home the long way around. With luck, we'd get to Nantes before the storm arrived tomorrow. If we left now, we could still take a look at the troglodyte areas near Les Elyzes de Tayac Sireuill, and then continue on D-706, a sinuous road that borders the river Vezere, and connect with highway A-89. Then, we could take A-20 toward Paris, and turn left on A-85 towards Nantes passing through Tours and Angers. This part of the trip would take us two days to complete.

Nevertheless, we finished breakfast in peace, packed our bag and said our goodbyes. We promised to come back. We tanked up at a supermarket gas station and settled on the cafe next to it to rest a bit.

Then our vacation stopped. The rest of the trip was a monotonous job that we simply had to complete. Back on the road, we went due north on D-704, and then D-62. After less than an hour, we took highway A-89 running east, and we soon connected with A-20. The plan was to follow A-20 passing Limoges—the town known for its expensive pottery—and then continue to Vierzon where we could connect with A-85, and head straight home.

Back on the highway, we're running toward Paris at conservative power settings. I planned to go for max range and only stop when I could hear the clattering of the valve train amplified by the nearly empty gas tank. Do not trust the low level fuel light on a Virago. Don't ask me how I know this.

I quickly assumed the fat, dumb and slow cruising position. I shuffled in the seat and adjusted my helmet. If I had had a window, I would have opened it and stuck my elbow out—but I didn't—so, with my left hand, I grabbed the base of the left mirror. Somehow this made me more comfortable and helped fight the wind. I wasn't driving anymore; I was just a passenger sitting behind my eyes, slowly falling into a state of suspended animation as the reassuring humming of the engine at 4000 RPM, provided a fitting background. My only worry was that my passenger might fall asleep and fall off the back.

Suddenly I was startled by the beep of a horn. It was a late model BMW GS, going by at nearly twice my speed, the driver, giving me the European salute by briefly extending his right leg. Ah, now I felt slow. Imagine yourself, sitting there in your open cockpit biplane with no heat, freezing while trying to get home before the storm gets you and turns you to bits, when suddenly an F-4 Phantom goes by and waves, barely hanging around for you to notice his matching helmets, matching suits, high-tech windshield and loads of onboard electronics—not to mention, heaters. Very nice, but I tried to console myself by affirming that I'm a purist and that I like to do things the old way, like a real man. This statement does a bad job of hiding the fact that my face was frozen due to the "old style" open face helmet I insisted on wearing and that I was too cheap to buy a new windshield, let alone a BMW GS.

As the time passed, and before the first hour mark, I was nearly immobilized by the cold. The low temperature, poor clothing, and my bad fitness condition didn't allow me to go for maximum range. I had to stop and warm up. We pulled in at the next station where, with all the grace of a recently revived Frankenstein, I filled up and pushed the bike to the parking slot in front of the cafe's front window.

Inside, Martine nursed a cup of hot chocolate, and I soon joined her. "Good thing we didn't come by car," I joked. Before leaving, we warmed our gloves and ourselves thanks to the pivoting nozzles of the powerful hand dryers in the bathrooms. We resumed the now familiar cruising routine: ride for a maximum of 45 minutes, and then stop to warm up.

We passed Limoges. Thankfully, there were no traffic jams. The city looked nice from the highway. Someday we'll come back. The sun set before 6 p.m. around here, and by then I'm done. As we reached Chateauroux, putting on the turn signal and rolling off the throttle, marked the end of the day—but not the problems.

I had a knot in my throat as I knew it might take more than an hour wandering around before we found accommodations. I negotiated the obligatory runabout then crossed the bridge over the highway and ... hallelujah! There, half a mile away, the bright lights and spotless white and yellow paint of a "Premiere Classe" Motel. I'm a lucky dog!

The young girl behind the desk put us in a room on the ground floor. We quickly unpacked and made plans to go to a restaurant nearby. After a good meal and a hot shower, we settled in to watch TV before falling asleep early.

The next morning, a thick, heavy fog covered the area. It had not rained but still the bike was wet. We took time enjoying our breakfast, and then prepared to leave. We put on every piece of clean clothes we had left: double T-shirts, long sleeves, special expensive cold weather motorcycle shirt, bandana, neck warmer, ski mask, and the rain suits.

It was past 9 a.m., and we still needed lights to get around as we were looking for gas. I wanted to get on the highway with a full tank. The storm almost caught us overnight and was getting serious—and cold. When I got back to the highway, I didn't see a sign with the name of our next big city, Vierzon, so I rolled the dice ... and lost.

We found ourselves going back the way we came and coming face to face with the storm front. It started to rain, and it was an agonizing seven miles before we could exit and turn around. Once pointing in the right direction, we tried to escape at 80 mph, rain suits flapping in the breeze. After 20 minutes, we're clear and could slow down. The sky opened up, and we could almost see the sun, but it was cold, and the menacing darkness was still there in the mirror.

The rest of the day was uneventful. We found A-20 and continued home, our cruising speed determined by the amount of rain suit flapping we could endure and our ability to withstand the progressively increasing cold ride. We finally got off the highway at Ancenis, and rode familiar roads to get home before sundown.

Once parked in front of our garage door, I fumbled for the big garage key—for a week, forgotten—in one of my jacket pockets. Martine left to go get the cat, and I was left alone in the garage.

I placed the bike on its centerstand, marking the end of our adventure. There was only one thing left to do: Start planning the next one.

But before that, all I wanted to do was take that final, long, hot shower and get some sleep. Our drifting was officially over ... until next year.

—Jorge Picabea

48. On the Road to Namibia

South Africa really is a great country for long distance rides. Having ridden on the back of my dad's bike out to the surrounding countryside of Johannesburg when I was growing up, I couldn't wait for the day when I would get the opportunity to do the same on my first bike, a red 2005 Hyosung GT 250.

My dad had also just got himself a blue 2007 Suzuki SV650S. It finally arrived when my family and their rather large group of friends organised a five day river rafting trip on the Orange River in Namibia. I'll never forget the expression I made when my dad said that we would ride there.

Over the months leading up to the trip, we went on practice runs to outlying small towns (colloquially known as dorpies) of which there seem to be an infinite number in South Africa. But finally the day came.

At six in the morning, we got our pannier bags on the bikes, geared up, got on our bikes, turned on the ignition and rode!

Johannesburg is approximately 1300 kilometres away from the particular part of the Orange River we were going to. The river forms part of the border between South Africa and Namibia. Not wanting to spend too much money, we would cover the distance in two days.

Everything was going smoothly. But if the trip was smooth the entire way, there wouldn't be a story to tell. Near the end of the day, I was coming out of a curve and changed to fourth gear. Then, abruptly, the clutch lever decided to flap against the handlebars uselessly. Fortunately we were just arriving in a town, and I pulled over fairly safely, stalling the bike in the process.

Both my dad and I feared the same thing—that the cable had snapped. A quick inspection revealed that the pin that held the engine end of the clutch cable had gone on its own trip somewhere behind us. With a very inadequate pair of side cutters, we nicked some wire from a farm fence I had pulled over next to, and twisted

197

so as to tie the cable to the actuator. (Two years later and that fix is still in place.)

Feeling elated with our victory over an MIA clutch pin, we set off again. Every hundred kilometres or so, the Suzuki's stone seat and vibrations from my bike would periodically turn our rears into jelly, and we would have to take a break whilst our rears transformed back into semi healthy flesh. It was at one of these breaks that my dad noticed something. The bolt that fastened the top of my exhaust to the Hyosung's tail had lost its nut and was hanging on by a thread—quite literally! I had done some maintenance before the trip—which in hindsight, must not have included looking at the exhaust bolt. I needed to have spent more time with my pre-ride checklist.

The engine oil cap had also started to come loose, and the bike had lost some oil.

But the worst part was the licence disk—which would normally sit between the bolt that held up my exhaust and the same nut that had dropped off several hundred kilometres behind us—had followed that nut. This disk would be a problem at the border post, where the license disk on a vehicle is ultimately more important than the number plate. Scavenging a bolt from my dad's bike and some good tightening, fixed the problems, but we could do nothing about the license disk.

I was extremely worried for the rest of the trip because, in the worst case scenario, we would have to leave the bike at either of the two border posts we would have to pass through and pray it was still there when we got back from the river rafting. I have not said this yet, but I love this bike. It's more than I could ever have asked for as a beginner's bike, and I would not have any other bike for my first bike. With the license disk missing, this could be my last ride on it!

Later that day, we were a hundred kilometres out from our overnight stop, Upington, and the license disk was the last thing on my mind. Having just passed through a town with a very large insect population, I found my visor showed more goo than road. After a solid day of riding fatigue, we found ourselves also looking through sun glare staring at the sunset. (After that incident, I don't know how all those cowboys in the movies could ride off into the sunset so calmly.)

We covered the last hundred kilometres to Upington in one stint. I don't know how my dad felt, but I was dreaming about the tall buildings—relative to the flat veldt around us—of Upington and all their glorious shade.

We booked into our bed and breakfast and went for supper at a nearby bar. (International travellers take note, whilst our currency sucks, B & B's are still much cheaper than hotels and will offer similar if not identical levels of accommodation.)

At the bar, we started talking with two other bikers, one of which told us about her husband's story in the northern parts of Africa:

> Her husband was with a large group of riders doing a tour of northern Africa. Now passing between countries in the rest of Africa is no small matter. The mountain of paperwork required to get 30 or so riders between all the countries they were touring was enough to fill a large book, so she said. In one country—she neglected to mention which—a single police officer-soldier-militia-man with a gun was giving them kak (I'm sure you can work out what this translates to) for not having something or other in order. He said that he would have to accompany the group whilst they detoured to some governmental facility in order to sort this out. The group leader was fairly certain that whatever this man was talking about was a load of bull. So, as the

indignant enforcer climbed on the back, the leader gunned the throttle, stood the bike on its rear wheel, promptly throwing off the enforcer. The leader took off with the rest of the group toward the border post, leaving the enforcer behind shaking his fists in the air.

Well, we headed back to our rooms and turned in. The next morning when we started on our second leg, I started noticing a strange feeling and sound. Whenever I would pull off, the bike would feel slow and seemed to bounce its way into moving. Instead of revving up nicely, the engine would oscillate before stabilizing, and then the bike would start accelerating properly. I didn't think much of it at first, but it got steadily worse and worse as the trip went on. The second leg wouldn't be as long as the first, and as we rode into Sbringbok, we met up with some of the family who were driving up from Cape Town.

On this trip, I had already learned a lot. One important lesson was that a 250cc motorcycle might not be the best machine for long distance touring. For the greater part of the trip, we had been travelling west, and the wind—that was with us the whole way—was pushing us to the left. Now that we had started north for Namibia, we were riding into the wind head-on. Even fully opening the taps didn't make the bike go any faster than 100 kilometres an hour in that wind. On one of our breaks, my dad said to ride behind him, so as to slipstream him. It was certainly one of the scariest parts of my riding experience, getting about a foot away from a large mass of moving rubber—hair raising, indeed. Mercifully, the wind lessened, and I could ride normally again. At the next fuel stop, my bike had gained an increase in mileage of about 50 percent from the slipstreaming.

We were getting very close to the border when we found a surprise. Up until now we had been riding on some of the flattest ground and straightest road we had ever seen. And just outside the South African side of the border post, there were some of the best corners and twisty sections imaginable. As we approached the border, I had become increasingly worried this would be my last ride on this bike. When I saw this section of road, I thought to myself: "If this is my last ride on this bike, I will damn well enjoy it!" So I sliced through those turns and had an absolute blast, and I was feeling on top of the world as we neared the border post.

Apparently, there was meant to be some sort of luggage check at the SA border post. Not so much as a batted eyelash as we handed in our papers and passed through, without a second glance. The Namibian border post was more of an old aircraft hangar than a border post. We saw a parking lot and then joined a queue to check our passports and papers. That's it. There wasn't even a gate to prevent anyone from simply driving straight through the border post. More likely than not, if we had simply parked, hung around the buildings a bit, gone inside and come out a few times we could have then simply driven through and no one would have noticed. But we were good. We handed in our papers and went in legally. There was no flinging of people off bikes here. And what about the bike's license? Not a word was said, either by us or the border patrol staff.

Almost immediately after we left the border post, we took our turnoff to the river rafting company. I'm going to summarise here: we rowed boats; we camped; we made music (in our family tradition); and we fell in the water.

Now, time to worry again, because we were going the other way through the South African border post. The Namibian border post was still more old aircraft hangar than border post, so I wasn't worried about that part.

This time at South African customs, we had our number plates taken down, and our license disks examined. They asked about my missing one, and we told them what had happened. My dad at the beginning of the trip very wisely decided to bring with us the proof of ownership forms for our bikes and the customs official casually glanced over these. He seemed satisfied and let us through the gate. That was it; the whole ordeal wasn't anything to worry about.

The ride home was uneventful, until we got to Johannesburg. By this time, that weird feeling that the bike had on the first leg was beginning to become a real problem. I talked to my dad about it, and we examined the chain. It was shot. It had stretched so much that it was making it difficult to pull off without stalling. Worse, it was still stretching. However, we agreed that we would wait and replace the chain when we got home.

Joburg drivers have a habit of pulling off very quickly when the light goes green, and one doesn't want to be caught up in the mess of impatient car drivers all trying to get home from work. Nevertheless, we made it home in one piece with our weak chain. My dad's trip meter counted a total of 2638 kilometres there and back.

Despite all the problems I had, I loved every moment of the trip, and while river rafting wasn't my thing, riding to see the family again, very much was.

—Jason Blundell

49. Never Seen Rain

Mister! I ride to live; I live to ride. When I'm not riding, I'm thinking about riding.

Reading the classified section of motorcycles for sale, I've seen ads in which the seller informs the potential buyer that the motorcycle has never been ridden in the rain and has always been stored in the garage. I smile to myself because an old Iron Butt Rider like me could never make such a claim.

I've ridden all of my bikes in the rain. When I do, I just power wash the bike after the ride, wipe it down, wax the paint, and polish the chrome obsessively.

I take care of my '03 as I would a good woman. Yeah, we are in love, and we've seen a little rain. Riding in the inclement weather is a result of fate as much as choice. Once the ride has started, I'm not going to let a little rain bring an end to our time together.

Our resolve has been tested more than a few times by the rain. And, I can assure you sir, I've ridden in the rain enough to know that I don't like it! Give me a woman who can two-up, put her rain gear on, and ride in the rain without complaining, and I will introduce you to the woman I love. Because she is the navigator and takes care of the reservations during the ride, I will cherish and adore this woman, forever. Yes sir!

The '03 and I have ridden some long distances together. We heard about this club called the Iron Butt Association. The only way into the club is to ride your way in with the shortest qualifying distance being 1000 miles in 24 hours. It was a commitment, but I thought that was cool.

I didn't know if I could do it, but I did, and after a while, we also successfully rode for the BunBurner Gold, a ride covering 1500 miles in 24 hours.

Like a long, satisfying love affair with a beautiful woman, the '03 and I have been enjoying our life together. We've been through some tough rides, but in the end our trust for one another has grown, and I'm about as happy as a man could ever be, just the '03, my woman, and me.

—Rick Tilbury

50. An Unlikely History of Motorcycles

April 1, 2005

I seem to recall being asked by the American Motorcycle Alliance (AMA) to write a short article on the history of motorcycles. Of course, this subject could fill many libraries since the motorcycle has served as our society's main transportation for the past 100 years. This is my attempt to condense all this to a few pages.

It's hard to imagine how we would have developed as a world power without our motorcycles.

The Harley-Davidson Motor Company, being our largest American company, is owed much credit for the standard of living we all have today. The founding of the Motor Company in 1903 occurred in the same year that many great inventions were introduced including crayons, the bottle making machine, windshield wipers, and the Wright brothers first gas motored and manned airplane. Of course, the Harley-Davidson motorcycle was the greatest invention of all.

In 1908, a Harley sold for $210. Mr. Henry Ford, an early automobile manufacturer, sold his popular Model T in 1908 for $950. Thus, the Harley motorcycle provided transportation at a much more affordable price.

In 1913, there was talk that Henry Ford was onto some new method of mass producing cars that would lead to a great reduction in price of the Model T. Some said it could result in a price below that of Harley's motorcycle.

As fate would have it, Ford got sick of the city life in 1913 and decided to move back to the country life where he was brought up and felt more comfortable. He was a friend of the Davidson brothers, and he decided to sell his complete operation to Harley-Davidson for enough money to finance his retirement. I guess we'll never know what Ford might have had up his sleeve for 1914.

With Ford's retirement, the Harley-Davidson Motor Company grew faster than it ever imagined. It quickly took over much of the available building space in Milwaukee. It hired all the Ford engineers and most of the engineers from competing automobile and motorcycle companies. America would henceforth grow using the transportation of the motorcycle.

Some of the ex-Ford engineers decided to use Ford's manufacturing methods and created an assembly line capable of turning out one motorcycle every 24 seconds. Harley-Davidson quickly patented the whole process thereby keeping other manufacturers from competing with them. After that, most car and motorcycle companies fell by the wayside as Harley-Davidson expanded its empire and influence.

Motorcycles had to adapt somewhat to be able to accommodate the American family. The sidecar was fitted to more than 60 percent of all new motorcycles. Special enclosures were developed to seal out bad weather. Roads began to improve to provide fast transit for the millions of motorcycles that were coming off the assembly lines in Milwaukee. The roads were built with widths just eight inches wider on each side of a complete sidecar rig. For bigger families, a tandem sidecar was produced that was rigidly affixed to the motorcycle. Suspensions developed that allowed the bike to lean around corners while the sidecar leaned with it. There were still many solo motorcycle riders. There was some concern about safety and riding in bad weather. The government stepped in and passed many laws to mandate special protective riding apparel and crash resistant motorcycles.

During wartime, domestic motorcycle production was cut back favoring military vehicles. The Harley-Davidson airplane became a potent force in winning the War with Europe in 1948-1952. President Davidson was president of the United States during that war. There was a slight scandal in 1949 when he was caught spooning with an intern in a sidecar near the Washington Monument.

After the War with Europe, Howard Hughes was hired to expand the Harley airplane. He found ways to build a giant Harley airplane made out of wood. Detractors called it the Spruce HOG (Harley Or Goose?). That idea didn't fly, and Hughes helped the Motor Company figure out how to turn milk into urine. They used the urine to make special ointment to put in the Harley first aid kits in case any riders got bitten by jellyfish while riding on the beach at the Daytona Rally.

By the early '80s, an upstart dropout from Harvard, Bill Gates, had built an experimental computer operating system he called DOS. Having no funding, he approached Willie G. Davidson for backing. Willie G. immediately saw the benefits of the new operating system to control all the proposed fuel injection modules Harley had planned for its motorcycles. He offered Gates one million dollars for the operating system patents and bought him out on the spot. Gates decided to return to Harvard where he became a full professor in Ancient Civilizations. Willie G. renamed the operating system as the HOG OS and created a new company to market it called MicroHOG. We all know how big that company is today. It produces 99 percent of all the computers and operating systems in the world and has provided all the hardware/software modules for every space mission.

Now, when you buy a Harley, you get a computer as a bonus. The computer is linked to an orbiting system of Harley satellites that send and receive signals to every motorcycle in the world. The Motor Company has complete control of the transportation system now by being able to monitor the location of every motorcycle.

Today, every house has a three-motorcycle garage. Every family has a motorcycle rig with as many as three seats in tandem. The motorcycle part of the rig has an enclosed sealed canopy for winter use. The canopy and sidecar are completely sound insulated with full airbags. The bike itself has an integral airbag and safety monitoring system. The Harley satellites are continuously monitoring every motorcycle for any safety violations. Upon receipt of any impending-accident signal from a bike, the GPS monitor sends distress signals to local law enforcement and ambulance services. Harley calls it the HOG-Star system. Highway monitors keep track of all vehicles and the state-of-the-art Motorcycle Movement System (MMS) allows for hands-free operation of sidecar rigs by depressing a single button on the motorcycle dashboard. Riders can still travel the roads using their own abilities but for long distance travel or other city-to-city travel, the bikes have the option to hook-up to MMS for automatic hands-free operation.

In 2005, the AMA has 200,000,000 members in the United States. In addition to controlling all aspects of the United States Transportation System (USTS), they provide motorcycle roadside services in case of breakdowns or dead batteries. They also plan road trips. The AMA is a subsidiary of Harley-Davidson.

The Motor Company produces exceptionally reliable and quiet engines. There have been some inquiries from Japanese manufacturers trying to market their Hondas and Yamahas here, but the import tariffs are so high that no outside company wants to sell here. It's probably a good thing since most of these foreign bikes have loud exhausts and are always breaking down on the European highways.

On our Motorcycles forums, we hear members from Europe wishing that they could purchase one of our Harley machines. Unfortunately, exports of Harleys are not allowed. There is so much USA demand that production is now done in 88 plants scattered across the country running three shifts a day.

Since the turn of the new century, Harley-Davidson has been slowly studying hydrogen fuel cell engines. Some hybrid motorcycles are also being studied that would use electric motors in addition to the regular V-Twin engines we have all come to know so well. Even the schools offer courses taught by Harley specialists in how to get ready for these new motorcycle technologies.

There is no need for any journalists to report on new Harley motorcycles. Harleys are readily available at reasonable prices from Wal-Mart stores. Repairs are minimal. When something does go wrong, a simple call to Wal-Mart brings a truck out to pick up the bike. They do the repairs and return the bike the next morning. The repair cost is automatically subtracted from your Wal-Mart paycheck. Sometimes they even throw in a new toaster as a good will gesture. Since almost everyone works either for Harley-Davidson (to provide for all your transportation needs) or Wal-Mart (to handle the rest), it makes for a great 2-company society.

The latest models produced by Harley-Davidson are the EL Knucklehead, the FLH, and the Sportster 883, that have stood the test of time since their introduction more than 50 years ago. Of course, they each come with a variety of sidecar rigs at higher cost. The new hydrogen fuel cell models are expected to be introduced sometime in the next century ...

"Walt ... Walt ... Wake up! ... You were mumbling something about hydrogen motorcycles and President Davidson with an intern. Have you fallen asleep watching Desperate Housewives again?"

"What? ... Oh my God, what a nightmare! I thought I was in a parallel universe there for a minute ... I guess it was just a bad April Fool's dream."

—Walter F. Kern

Acknowledgments

I would like to thank my late wife, Jane Ann Cunning Kern, who spent 47 years with me before her untimely and tragic death in 2008. She observed me trying one thing after another looking for my destiny. I had always liked to write but never found a good outlet until I joined About.com in 1999. There I had to develop complex skills of building a Website from scratch while generating original content on a regular basis. Fortunately, the site was called Motorcycles, my passion. Jane took up motorcycling with me by getting trained and buying her own bike in 1989. We traveled everywhere together, joined many motorcycle groups, and met hundreds of people from all over the world, either in person or on the Internet. She enjoyed the fact that near the end of my stay at About.com, it was acquired by the New York Times. She never lived long enough to see my first book on motorcycling come out in 2011. This current book, an anthology, is my second book. Hopefully, she's looking down as I continue writing about things that bring joy to my new life.

About the Author

Walter Kern spent 35 years as an electrical engineer for Bell Laboratories. After he had retired in 1996, he built Websites for a while and then signed on at About.com as its Motorcycles Guide. There he started with a 3-page site and built it into one with more than 20,000 pages. After leaving About.com in 2007, he founded the Motorcycle Views Website (motorcycleviews.com). He also manages the Polar Bear Grand Tour Website (polarbeargrandtour.com) and takes all their weekly pictures. He took up motorcycling at the age of 51 together with his wife, Jane, who also rode her own motorcycle. Jane died in 2008 as a front seat passenger in an automobile accident. Walter currently rides a 2000 Honda Gold Wing SE Motor Trike, is a pet parent to an eight-pound Maltipoo watchdog named Princee and writes a lot at a new home in Florida with his fiancée, Rosemarie.

Made in the USA
Middletown, DE
31 December 2018